# Make Every Day Father's Day

## By Being There

### Theodore Wentz

**author**HOUSE®

AuthorHouse™
1663 Liberty Drive
Bloomington, IN 47403
www.authorhouse.com
Phone: 833-262-8899

Teddy Bear Publishing
PO Box 82
Mount Pocono, PA 18344

Published by AuthorHouse  07/29/2022

ISBN: 978-1-4490-5754-1 (sc)
ISBN: 978-1-4490-5755-8 (hc)
ISBN: 978-1-4490-5756-5 (e)

Library of Congress Control Number: 2010900969

# Table of Contents

# Acknowledgements

Writing this book was a true mixed bag of emotions, memories of the woman called Mom, and what she had to do to raise seven kids herself, and the wonderful job her daughter-in-law did as a eighteen year old wife and a nineteen year old mother. We were determined to give our kids the best opportunity we can with as much love as possible. For Loretta to accept my proposal and marriage and the sacrifices of young adulthood was really a challenge. It was a job well done. To Lanard, Terrance, and Ashley, thank you. May you please continue to shine bright in this world, there is nothing easy about doing the right thing, but it's the only way to go. To my many personal heroes, both men and women whose shoulders I stand, thank you. Again, to Harold my big brother, thank you for your leadership and the sacrificing of your youth to lead six of your younger siblings through the rough and tough sixties and seventies, while mom worked two jobs to see to it we had a roof over our heads and food in our mouths. We spent many a night wondering if we were going to make it from one day to the next. As phony as it may sound, I truly thank God. Only he knows how hard it was for mom to keep five boys and two daughters focused and in line. I remember on Thursday nights, she would march us, one by one, in front of our friends playing in the streets of Brooklyn and Queens going to service with our suits and ties on. May the readers of this book feel the passion of our experience and believe just as we did that the only person that can stop you is you yourself. Please don't let it happen. Be a "Be there Father and Mother", it's not as hard as you may think.

Thank You

Theodore L. Wentz

# Foreword

"I wish young people could just skip over the years between 10-23... either that or sleep through those years. All that happens during that time is getting girls pregnant, hurting old people, stealing and fighting" Shakespeare, A Winter's Tale

When I was asked to write the forward to "Make Every Day Father's Day" my initial response to my friend was "I'm no expert on children". I am a doctor but children are not my specialty. He countered by reminding me of my rich experience as a mother, grandmother, an advocate for children/adolescents, in addition to my professional experience treating adolescents. I said okay. It is difficult to say no to Teddy.

Make Every Day Father's Day, is a heart felt, common sense book with recurring themes that makes so much sense that one may wonder why any one thought they needed to be penned by a working class man, without any prior writing experience. Teddy would be the first to say he's no expert on child rearing, but everyone who knows him knows that he's had a lot of child rearing experience. He helped raise his five younger siblings, his older brother modeled for him, all this before he became a husband and a father. He has been a hands on Dad to his three children. His goal- never to have them experience the deep sadness he felt because his father was not in his life.

There are several points that are made using probably little known data that makes it apparent why Teddy wrote this book, aside from celebrating his beloved mother. Besides the fact that there are several thousand children in foster care and uncounted numbers in single head of household families, and thousands more in jails and prisons raised without fathers, it becomes apparent how a man raised without his father, watching his mother struggling to raise seven children became passionate about men being there for their children. Behind every statistic is a person with their own story, this is Teddy's.

A few of the recurring, common sense themes, some repeated many times in different ways are very basic, but not followed far too frequently.

*Adolescents/adults, once you become a parent, it is your responsibility to take care of your child no matter what—that means both parents,

*Don't have unprotected sex unless you are ready to be a parent.

*We all have choices, visualize the end result of the choice you are about to make, so that you will make the right choice.

*You don't have to make all the mistakes possible …life is too short.

Learn from others.

*Don't limit yourself, challenge yourself, stay focused.

*Education is the great equalizer.

*God, family and community are the formula for success.

Teddy dedicated the book to his late mother. As a religious person myself I would be surprised If Teddy didn't have an occasional spiritual or emotional conflict; since the scripture clearly admonishes us "to have no other God before me". You will feel the love, the admiration and almost deification of his mother as you read his book.

The world has benefited from her steadfastness, and devotion to her family. She raised five sons and two daughters without their father. The men in their religious congregation were often available to help her with the boys, but given Mrs. Russell's beauty, I feel fairly certain they were willing to help with the children and any other needs she may have had. Her sacrifices paid off, not just for her children, but her grand children, and the community. In fact, the expectation, and admonition always was that one was to be "a credit to your community". Part of the training to be a contributor to your community was to learn discipline. She taught her children discipline. She taught by example, working two jobs, maintaining her home, she taught them by reasoning, but when words weren't enough she didn't spare the rod. Oh, there are today's modern parents who will frown on the rigorous discipline she meted out, and later her children used on their children as well. But the thing speaks for itself.

Part of her teaching related to respecting women. I have not read, seen or heard women spoken of with such reverence maybe ever, as in this book. We are a protected class.

This book contains information that many may say they already know. To know and to do are different. We need to know the principles, not only know but internalize them, process them then let them guide our way. If we do, we can even prove Shakespeare wrong. Children are not a problem that we should hope they sleep from age 10 to 23. They are our most precious resource. They need both parents, grand parents, the schools, the religious congregation, the village to nurture them. I hope this book will become required reading for adolescents so that every day in fact becomes children's day, mother's day and father's day because we are all in this together.

Forward by Roxie Mae. Editing by Theodore Wentz.

# Being There

It was the seventh day of March, 1979 Loretta had early morning labor pains. I took her to her mother's house in route to work because the doctor told us during one of our visits that when labor starts, a mother with her first child would be in labor for four to six hours. After nine AM, I called his office and he said monitor the contractions. When they become every fifteen to thirty minutes consistently, and if they get stronger, longer, and closer together, bring her in. The doctor also wanted her to walk around as much as possible. Since I only worked twenty minutes away when I got the call, I left work and ran to Loretta's mother's house. Loretta was in true labor and surprised the doctor for being in true labor with her first child, and within four to five hours. The doctor wanted us to meet him in his office instead of going straight to the hospital, which I thought was odd. When we arrived at his office, Loretta's mother came with us. This was her family's first grandchild, and my families second. The doctor was away from his office delivering another child. While in the office, his nurse asked me to have Loretta lay on the table so when he arrives she will be ready for delivery. Seconds turned into minutes, minutes turned into hours. I was never a heavy coffee drinker, but that day I was drinking coffee black. The future grandmother, who had a medical background, was getting restless. The doctor's nurse kept calling for him, but his patient was having complications delivering which delayed him to our delivery. When he finally arrived, I thought Loretta's mother was going to jump on the doctor. Little did she know I would have beaten her to it. He asked me to take down her garments while he was changing into his uniform. Portions of the Amniotic Sac were protruding, and as soon as the doctor broke the water, our first-born literally jumped out of his mother into the doctors arms. This was to be the first of three challenging yet great experiences; all three of the children's births were truly a gift from God. I held our first born within seconds of his birth. While his mother was being stitched up, I was holding him in a blanket counting his fingers and toes, praying that everything else was normal with our first child. This was a young man born to a mother who was raised in a nice middle class family, three aunts and one uncle, a family who believed in God, and was a credit to their community. A mother who graduated from school six months early, began working as a young teenager babysitting for neighborhood working mothers and began traveling in and out of Manhattan while working in a lawyer's office at seventeen. When I met Loretta and her family on February 5, 1977, she was seventeen going on eighteen and just out of high school. Her mother worked at a local hospital and her father worked for the New York City Transit Authority. I was twenty-two, graduated from high school at seventeen, six months early, and made the honor roll as a junior. My co-operative program grades were good enough to work a week and go to school a week through out the school year. I exceeded the thirty-two credit requirement to graduate. Coming from a broken home (my father and mother separated when I was ten years old), I began working at the tender age of ten cutting grass and shoveling snow in the neighborhood. At age thirteen, I was allowed to be a Daily News paperboy. I apologize for pausing; wiping away tears remembering my mother working waking me up to make me breakfast and sending me out to start my route at five in the morning on Sundays. At age sixteen, I was allowed to work at McDonalds after school until eleven pm, sometimes later as long as I did well in school. I sacrificed a lot to work; I made every junior high and high school basketball team but chose to work and help my mother out instead. I might add, while making my little $54 a week at age thirteen, I would give everything to her, just to find it returned to me in an envelope on my nightstand the next morning. I guess the thought to her made all the difference in the world. I painted portions of our house with my older brother at age seventeen, between June and September of

1972. After helping my older brother, I took my younger brother with me to paint houses on our block. We painted four houses on our block alone. That summer my older brother asked me, quote, "kid, what are you doing"? I responded "nothing". He asked me to come with him down to New York City's office of Personnel to file for city employment, and that is exactly what I did. I filed for New York State employment, received 9.25 on the test and began working for New York State Board of education, the next summer at age 18. I stayed in public service for the state of New York, and then for the City of New York. I worked for the New York City Transit Police Department Special Services Bureau for the next twenty-one and a half years. Therefore, a special thank you to you Big Bro, and to my mother, to whom this book and my life is dedicated too. It is also dedicated to all of the great strong women of all colors, races, and creeds, who did what was necessary to raise their families alone. In addition, to you great strong be there fathers as well, this book is dedicated to you. My mother was born and reared in Charlotte North Carolina, lost her parents early in life (father at age thirteen, mother at sixteen), and had to help raise her younger siblings. She never finished school. She was married to my father at eighteen, had her first child at nineteen, and me two days before her twenty-second birthday. This woman was a rare person whom God put here on earth to be anything that she wanted to be. She was a beautiful woman who was able to sing. As a teenager, when we walked down the street, people thought she was my girlfriend. This woman sacrificed everything for her children and raised seven of us by herself, with the help of members of our congregation, and God himself. Many of the brothers in the congregation would study the Bible with us and treat us like their own children. To all of them, many thanks. My father served in the Korean War from 1951 to 1953 and made sergeant first class. He was a chef in the military and later worked at one of the top rated seafood restaurants in the great city of New York City, Oscars. He also was a car salesman. Lanard was born to four uncles and two aunts on my side of the railroad tracks. After my father and mother separated in the early sixties, my older brother Harold became Big Brother and Chief in his early teens while mom became full time provider for our family. Harold, thank you on behalf of all of your younger siblings. Thank you for giving up your youth for the responsibility you were given, not by choice but by necessity. I would not be writing this book if it wasn't for your leadership and sacrifice in helping six of your siblings make it this far. God bless you from the bottom of my heart. Oh yes, and now back to my first born, Lanard was a normal child, nothing out of the ordinary. He was the only grandchild on his mother's side, and he was able to see his great uncle Limey Gibbs (who unfortunately died months after he was born) and he was the only great, great grandchild on his mother's side. That gave his great, great grandmother much joy and happiness before she died due to cancer in South Carolina. Being the second grandchild on my side and oldest and only grandchild on his mother's side, he was getting very spoiled. While at our regular religious meetings, I noticed a member in my congregation and his wife. They had three lovely daughters; they sat like little angels and never made a sound for two hours. I could not believe their good behavior, so one Sunday I asked them (their names were Vernon and Jo Ann) "I've been watching your girls for months, please tell me what is it that you do to make them behave so quietly every week". They thanked me for the compliment, and told me simply "Teddy, after they turned ten months old, when they did not listen, their little backsides got it and after a while, they got the message". As Lanard grew, and started using a baby seat, I took Vernon and Jo Ann's advice of loving him but giving tough love if needed. Moreover, to his mother, my wife, I thank her for allowing me to bring that type of discipline to our household. This was a woman who dated a man with her mother and father's approval at the age of seventeen and a half, and allowed her to be engaged at eighteen (twenty-one for me). In fact, we were engaged on her eighteenth birthday. Eight months after that we were married. In fact, her father caught me on my knees on their porch proposing to her. I will never forget what he said, "Get up off your knees"! I later bought her the engagement ring of her choice. She became pregnant at the age of eighteen and a mother at age nineteen, all while married to a broke husband. All we had was love and two great families to help us through. That was very hard for a nineteen year old who only had one boyfriend before meeting me and getting married all within fourteen months. My wife and I worked; at times, I worked two eight-hour jobs that totaled eighty hours a week. I began working two full time jobs while helping my mother with my brother and sisters in 1976, one year before meeting my wife. Thank you Loretta for getting out there and helping me, you did not have to. While growing up, Mr. Lanard (our first-born) experienced two hernia operations. The first at age ten months and a second at age three years old. He being the only child for two years and nine months, his mother did not let him out of her sight, even when her father wanted to take him to South Carolina without her. I was smart enough to stay out of that conversation, quietly rooting for our only child to stay put. Her mother and father understood and went south without their oldest and only grandson. Keeping in mind the ten month rule (beginning tough love), Lanard was approaching his ten months on this earth. We loved him yet made sure he behaved himself while at the babysitter or when we went out to dinner. Also remembering when we were at home with my mother, she raised five boys, so she was always spanking somebody. Once we became young teenagers, she would have us to go outside, take a long vine off one of our large bushes, strip the leaves off of them, and you know the rest. Lanard was too young for that, but that was at the back of my mind. I thought why not make sure that when our son needed a tanning on his bottom; make sure he got the point. I did not like hitting kids; I did not like hitting my younger siblings. He was truly a good child, spoiled and wanting to be picked up, but he understood that mommy and daddy's yes meant yes and no meant no. Between the years of 1979 through 1982, Lanard got his discipline when needed, but understood its better to listen to mom and dad than being spanked. After completing the seventies, we are now in 1981. We were horseback riding in upstate New York with other members of the congregation when my wife told me that she was feeling nauseated. It was early May; Sonny (Lanard) had just turned two years old. We did not trust the pregnancy test that much, so we decided to get check out. We were now beginning to go out again to dinner and such. As the summer progressed, the days turned into weeks and weeks turned into months. Loretta's nausea was happening more frequently, so we decided to go to the doctor. We did not trust pregnancy test that much, so we decided to go to the doctor. By June of 1981, after three months of wondering, our doctor congratulates us and says we were going to have a December 25th Christmas baby. Talk about a long hot summer. While waiting for our first child two years earlier, Loretta would come up to my job and we would do little things like window shop at the mall, buy baby clothes, take walks, visit family, etc. Likewise, while waiting for our second I would leave my day job, take a class or two (I worked at a college) then either go home to my family or on days that I did not have a class, pick them up so they could stay with me while I worked extra hours. I learned that if you sleep with a woman unprotected, there is a possibility that she might get pregnant. Having unprotected sex is for

*Grandpa and Grandma celebrate their 18th anniversary. They recently celebrated number 50. Let's all give them a big shout out! March 24, 1977.*

grown responsible adults who understood that when you make a baby, you must stay there and be the mother and father that child deserves. I learned that although unexpected, two children that my wife and I had did not ask to come in this world, and it was important to be in a committed relationship, like a marriage. We made it through the summer and fall, and now we were in the winter of 1981. Approaching Thanksgiving and Christmas, we bought more baby clothes, more maternity clothes, and more black coffee for me and stress medication, just kidding. Loretta grew impatient and I was there to comfort her (I give a big shout out to all you mothers, God bless you all). I was also fortunate enough to take the Lamaze classes to be there for all three of our children; thank you Paris and Juanita very much. Ms. Loretta grew very impatient as the due date drew near; we were hoping for the holiday season of our married lives. As we approached the twenty-fifth day of December, there were no signs of labor or anything. The due date came and went, then came mass hysteria! I'm trying to stay focused and Loretta wanted to know what is going on. I believe we even called the doctor. She was very comforting and said "day to day now". We were approaching New Years and I am praying to God "please don't let this baby past the first of the year because if that happens, I might need a hospital bed right next to her myself". Wouldn't you know it, December 31st, someone is getting mild labor pains. Nothing serious yet but we will take it. This looked like it was going to be our best New Year yet. We watched Dick Clarke bring in the New Year. Even though the labor was mild, we were directed to meet the doctor at the hospital that morning. While there, we walked and walked. Mr. Terrance decided he was ready to meet both his mother and father in the early afternoon of the first of January 1982. Not without a little drama of course. You see, while in labor, when Loretta's contractions were coming every fifteen to thirty minutes, she was asked to lie down so that the baby could be monitored. On the monitoring machine, which was used to watch the baby's heartbeat, the nurse and I watched. Loretta was in pain and I requested that the doctor come to us. During this, Ms. Loretta was reminding me that it was my fault that she was having labor pains. The nurse didn't think the doctor was needed. I said to myself "she is the nurse, what do I know"? While watching the monitor, I noticed my son's heart rate was fading. I remembered at our Lamaze classes that at this stage the baby's heart rate should be and remain strong right through the birth. I again alerted the nurse, she said not to worry and that everything was fine. I was shocked and confused, and I said to myself "I don't have time to argue with her". I strongly told the nurse "we had a tough experience with our first one and we don't want to take any chances. I'm paying you, the doctor, and the hospital. Call the Doc". She did. When the doctor arrived, she noticed the monitor and said, "Oh my God, this baby is in distress". I had to push my wife across the hall and I couldn't put on my hospital uniform cap and shoes. The Doctor proceeded to deliver our child; he had the umbilical cord around his neck. We almost lost him. Yes, that to this day was the happiest New Year for our family. Needless to say, my mother wanted charges bought against the hospital but I declined. I was just happy to have my healthy baby to see him grow up. And grow up he did, all six feet ten inches of him. Every year when he has his birthday, I remember that situation. You would think after two nerve-racking experiences like that, we would have given-up on having any more children, but not us. She wanted a daughter and I without a doubt wanted my little girl. The last young lady I helped spoil was my little sister Maria. The only thing we found out later during the course of Loretta's next pregnancy was that we had one more opportunity for our girl, which we will discuss when we get to Miss Ashley. Terrance, our second child, was an active child. He was the busiest baby I had ever seen. Not only was he busy, but his twenty two year old mother and his twenty-five soon to be twenty six year old father were very fortunate that we had him. His mom and dad had to regroup and start all over again with a baby that deserves both mom and dad in his life. To the young men and women reading this book; please, please think about the seriousness of having children. The lives of these children are at stake, once they are here, they're here, and you can't send them back. There is a national debate about abortions, not having an abortion simply because you had unprotected sex and did not mean to get pregnant. All I can say ladies and gentleman that there is only one sure way to not have unwanted children, and that's (I'll let you finish the sentence, if you can't, don't have sex at all). These two children of ours were both born to two people who were in a committed relationship. It also helps for the father to be there in case of an emergency. Now back to my busy little son Terrance. This young man enjoyed being the baby for almost six years, five years and eleven months to be exact. I had to learn to share my wife with a new child, and now our oldest child had to learn to share his mommy with a new brother. Of course, I was completely out of the picture with two young ones. With two struggling parents with two little ones, it took every penny and everybody there for us. It really took a village to make it work. I had to go out and get another full time job. I worked eighty hours a week until we felt that others could watch the baby. Then, Ms. Loretta went out and made it happen, sharing

*Dad and his boys.*

the financial responsibility. Thank you again, you didn't have to do it but did. Another point to my young readers, it wouldn't hurt for young men to be educated to be the best provider you can for your family. The mother of the child deserves to have a choice to just be a mom or she may choose to get out and help feed the family, a lesson our children grew-up and learned. I also believe young ladies should get a higher education as well; it benefits the children when both parents are there together for the kids. With the help of my wife and family, we were able to work, raise two kids, and be regular members of our congregation. Being close to God helped balance our lives as well. I was able to see other young parents struggle and make it, aside from that, I applied my ten-month rule of taking care of that backside if necessary. Mr. Terrance was very out-going. Being the second child, mom and dad began our perfect parenting. With our first child, we were very clingy. Lanard only went to the babysitter when necessary; with two children, we begged for a babysitter to have some "us" time. This is when it's good to have plenty of female sisters-in-law and a great set of parents- in-law. They were beyond perfect. Thank you Mr. Bill, Ms. Lucille, Mr. Phyllis, Debra, and Tweet. I will always love you folks to the end of time. Thank you! When you begin to make progress on your finances and another beautiful child decides to come, you have to take care of them no matter what. We Enjoyed limited vacations; despite the struggle we enjoyed each other when possible, but it was one thing I really learned, and that was "the woman is the most incredible creation to man". For my mother to have raised seven children by herself, and for my wife and other women to carry a child within them for nine months, be the main caregiver to the kids, and then get out and work side by side with us men, and still come home and cook, clean, and take care of the house finances, "where did you women come from"? Men of the world listen up. Momma, I wish you were here to read this written dedication to you. Loretta and all of you great women out there, on behalf of all of us men, those who appreciate and those who don't appreciate you, thank you and God bless you. The next year, 1983, we were at a religious function where we saw young pre-school kids sing a religious song and recite all the sixty-six books of the bible. I knew I had to get my son in this pre-school program at age four if it killed me. I begged my wife to work with me to pay out of own pockets to send him; she reluctantly agreed because we were still struggling but I said to myself that each of us are only four years old once and we need to just go for it. We did and the school worked with us for Lanard, and later Terrence as well. Thank you Mr. and Mrs. Green. Shout out to the New World Educational Center. While Lanard attended pre-school, his mom taught him how to read and write while I helped him with math. He progressed so well that before the end of the school year, he was already in first grade studies. The school was truly a great benefit to his future learning. He completed the pre-school program and was able to recite every book in the bible, and he was able to recite it backwards. I attended church regularly from age three, and getting through the first five books of the bible gave me trouble. The following September of 1984, he started kindergarten and continued to progress well in first grade. Mr. Terrence grew well also as a two year old. As I reflect on those hard but time well spent, sometimes I pinch myself remembering that at age eighteen I wondered what it would be like to be a father and married given what I

*The person who is my number 2 hero, Harold Wentz*

been through as a kid. I also wondered if there could ever be the perfect family, like the "Brady Bunch" or "Leave it to Beaver". I didn't have a "Cosby Show" in those days to relate to; sometimes I didn't know where to begin to be a good father. My father had long been gone. My older brother had just gotten married and I was next in line to be big brother and chief. I was being courted to go away to do religious work, but decided to stay back to assist the greatest mother ever to walk the Earth. This woman sacrificed everything like millions of women before her, with five younger siblings, and with mom being the only parent, I started my Public Service career with the State of New York. Mom and I worked well together. My older brother left a good legacy; we all knew what to do and we pretty much did it. I finally figured out the family I wanted. A hard working, well raised woman who was God fearing and wanted children. I wanted three kids, two boys and a girl with the girl to spoil. Girls are special; I certainly put my share in helping spoil our baby sister Maria. My late sister Chantel, another person this book is dedicated to, was strong minded but a wonderful sister. I believed I needed to stay home; perfect my big brother skills, work with mom, and learn everything I could from the brothers in the congregation. I also believed not to make any babies before I was married. I was not ready mentally or financially. I kept telling myself to be a sponge and soak in as much knowledge as possible. I said that by age twenty-five I should be ready for marriage. Oh well, so much for that goal. I was three years and one month early. By the year 1985, all was well. The kids were growing, and my younger brother had two boys also, and every time we would see them, my wife kept asking them "isn't it time for you to have that girl"? My brother had gotten married before we did in 1975; and had the oldest grandson and the third oldest grandson. They kept saying that they were finished. Then it hit me like a ton of bricks, whenever someone keeps telling other people why not go for a girl, maybe, just maybe, my wife is ready for her girl. I always told my brother's wife that. In comes 1986. I had taken a test for a better paying job with the New York City Transit Police Department Special Services Division. They called me for an interview in February of 1986; I accepted the position and transferred over from the State of New York to the City of New York. My time on the job carried over with that promotion. We wanted to grow-up with our kids. The having a girl talk heated up, we figured after I make probation and then a year after that we'll try to save some money. Wouldn't you know it, guess who got pregnant in March of 1987? I'll give you one guess. So we look at each other and say, "here we go again". Let's hope this is our girl! If you recall, I spoke of drama with our two sons earlier with their deliveries. This young lady decides to give us her version of drama. For the first three months of her mother's pregnancy, it wasn't if, but when we would lose her. I worked nights with the Transit Authority and it seemed that my two nights off, and a third night, we were either at or prepared to go to the hospital. At that time, our second son was enjoying his pre-school experience from the fall before and our oldest was in the second grade. So we had a lot of things happening at once. Once again young readers, when problems arise, daddy must be involved in the mother's life just in case of an emergency that requires a mature relationship and the support from each other. This is the responsibility of both parents with support from both families. The grandparents should be there to help the parents if needed, not the grandparents making the decisions the parents should be making. Thankfully, for us, the next five to six months were fairly stable with her. However, we did receive some bad news; if successful, this would be our last child. We couldn't have anymore; it would be medically unsafe. Needless to say, that made this pregnancy very special yet very nerve racking. Her mother holding on to her was key, which became a nightly prayer. To add insult to injury, our recommended doctor didn't know how to spell "Bedside manners". He knew his business medically, but needed to go to personality school. It seemed like our prayers paid off over the summer into the fall because we were in the safety zone. My wife turned twenty-eight and was ready to have her third child, God willing, with no more unexpected mishaps with this baby. Summer turned to fall and as we approached winter, my long lost father was approaching his fifty-eighth birthday. Little did we know that his oldest granddaughter would arrive on that very day. December came in very quietly. When told we were expecting our third child, we were given the month of December. I don't remember what date, no false labor, nothing dramatic. I had gotten off of work that morning of December 9th, went to run a few errands and do a cleaning job. We started a cleaning company in 1985 and we did jobs to supplement our income. Then I got the call; I immediately called my neighbor across the street to "please take her to the hospital and I would meet her there". I told my client about my wife being taken to the hospital. They understood, gave us their blessings, and off I went. When I got there, Loretta was already prepared to give birth. The Doctor said "Mr. Wentz, how much will you give me if this is a girl"? I said $100.00. He said "Where's my money, you have your girl". Her mother screamed; I jumped up and down! We couldn't believe it, a healthy baby girl. After the girls were comfortable, I of course called our parents and friends; people knew that this was our last chance to have a child. We were very happy. I couldn't tell my father because I didn't know where he was, but he was later informed. This was truly a happy day! My second child was born on January 1st, on my grandfather's birthday on my mother's side, and my daughter was born on December 9th, my father's birthday. With all of the struggles, trials, and tribulations, this really made it worth it, first have a child, and second have a healthy wife, and three healthy children in nine years and nine months. Now to continue with the ten-month discipline rule, hard work and tough love with children is always a blessing from God. But raising them correctly and being there was just as important. Having my mother and father-in-law, and one of my top five heroes, to call on was a great comfort. As we adjust to three children and the struggles that lie ahead, I said to myself when you expect your children to listen to us and do the right thing, what if they ask me "Dad, you want us to listen to you, you want us to progress in school, you want us to avoid the temptations of making dumb mistakes, tell us about your past and your youth". So as a twenty two year old father, I wanted to be able to expect the best from my kids, and to live by example myself. I began evaluating my life before I had children, during the course of having children, and the kind of husband I was and should be. When faced with such scrutiny, how would I standup? So I began to challenge myself, I thought long and hard of my past, my pre-school years, my school years, my accomplishments and failures, and added them up. To use a metaphor by President Bill Clinton, "I was where I was". Where do I go from age one to thirty two years of age? I would rate myself a passing grade of seventy-five; to me that was a complete failing grade. Passing was an eight-five percent or higher. I saw areas to improve as a husband, father, and as an overall person. What to do? First, take the information from my congregation more seriously; apply as many of God's principles as humanly possible. Listen to the rules of being a husband, a father and a mom who takes life more serious. I began self-evaluation regularly, learning from as many good people as possible. I asked parents of older children, men that were married longer, etc. To ask my children to walk the walk, I myself would have to walk that walk as well. I was quickly learning that being a father in a committed relationship was much harder than I thought, especially when you are trying to do the right thing. There are many distractions, many temptations, dealing with my own problems, problems with my wife, pressure at work, money issues, and having to spend every dime wisely. It left little space for error. One of the first mistakes I made was "Don't ever date with intention of marriage unless you can afford to have the option of the mother of your kids to stay at home". That is her option. Number two, have all of your financial ducks in a row. Number three, allow yourself twenty-five years to at least grow-up and mature. Understand what the true meaning of being a man is, and be one. Number four, I don't have to tell a man how wonderful sex is, but have it in a loving and committed marriage, because there is always the possibility of children. I'm not being a sex therapist, I'm thinking about the children. There is always a possibility of children. Number five, be responsible. Unprotected sex can cost you your life. You must ask yourself, "Is it worth it"? After getting a deadly disease, it is too late. Ladies, the mother of my children was a young lady who feared getting pregnant. She thought of the consequences. She, like all of you young ladies, had needs but she was a young responsible woman. That to me was the most beautiful trait. She was a lady. She got it honestly from her mother; her mother is still very much a wonderful lady herself. And so are her three younger sisters. They are truly a wonderful family. And she has a wonderful brother and father. Reflecting on how my mother was involved in every aspect of our lives growing up, I wondered if that was the way to go. You have to strike a balance, and you must start early. Loretta and I always found time to be in our kid's lives. Their mother liked animals, so she got our oldest son a dog. She always had cats, and I said to myself that people always reward dogs if they did something favorable, but never rewarded their children when they did something well. When the kids passed their exams, when they kept good attendance at school and moved on to the next grade, I thought that was reason to celebrate and get an extra McDonald's toy or

*Daddy and his girl*

lunch. Don't forget, we didn't have a lot of money, but we had a lot of love. When you don't have money, it forces you to be creative. Trust me, I've learned to make money and not let money make me. Money is a means to an end, not a defining characteristic. You can have money I'm told, but it can destroy you but you must keep your feet on the ground. My wife gave me a lot of wiggle room to work with, she had a slight different approach but it didn't totally disagree with mine. Failing was not an option, being left back wasn't an option, being bad in school was not an option. Although I would cut some classes to sneak to Coney Island, I cut only the classes I was passing and did it near the end of the school year. My mother had five to six kids in school at any given time. So I certainly didn't want to put any extra burden on a woman juggling so many balls at once. I made sure that she didn't get too many complaints from my teachers. So I advise all parents to start early involvement in their lives; homework, sports, anything that they might be interested in. Our mother allowed my older brother and me to play the saxophone, alto and tenor saxophone when we were in elementary school. In fact, it was around the time when President Kennedy was assassinated in 1963. I remember lugging a big saxophone back and forth from school. When a child is used to tough love early in their lives, by the time they begin looking you in your eye as a young adult, there will be no hitting back or swearing, and very little back talk. By the time we were teenagers we would run from our mother when we got her angry. My mother actually gave one of us a beating the day before we got married. The cliché or expression "this will hurt me more than it will hurt you" is something that I truly believe, because I hated spanking my kids. So I made sure I didn't have to do it often. They took me very seriously. With the boys, their mother would say, "I'm going to tell daddy", and they would stop on a dime. And when I got home, they still got some kind of dealing with. Our daughter was almost too shy for any kind of discipline. The ten-month rule applied to her as well. She grew up very well; she had a little friend named Mi-Mi, a neighbor's little girl who was also a well-raised and well-mannered young lady. They got along well and played

17

everyday together. When Loretta took sometime off to be with our daughter, her job literally begged me to convince her to come back to work, but I explained to her employer that in our family, our kids come first. We missed the income, but that was the case with her two other children. The first few months were very important to their growing up and connecting with their mother. Ashley was a very quiet, shy child. She still is very quiet; she was our miracle baby. The nine month process was quite nerve racking for the first three, and what made it more dramatic was the fact that we had one last chance to have her due to medical considerations. Fortunately, none of our kids had any long-term medical problems. Lanard and Terrance were doing well in school, and with the ten-month rule and tough love, we had no complaints. After our religious meetings on Sundays, we would at times go to lunch or brunch. The kids would sit nicely in their seats. Ashley at the time was in her high chair; some restaurant goers would stare at the kids. They never said anything to us but they would always watch the kids. I never said anything about it to their mother, but I kept it in the back of my mind. Time had passed and I believe we were at either Friendly's or our favorite restaurant Three Brothers. A person walked over to our table and said, "Your children are so well behaved". That caught us by surprise; we of course said thanks and thought nothing of it. I never counted, but we received that compliment from strangers often, even at our religious functions. I began to pay more attention to other families with young children to see if there were any differences with other families. Generally, most of the kids with their parents were well behaved. At our meetings, they would have to sit through two-hour sessions with periodic little walks. To help them sit quietly at our meetings, they would practice at home sitting still. Children will test you, they will see just how far they could go or get away with. I know I did. But mom changed all that. Raising children takes a lot of love and commitment; you must be dedicated to the long-term. For that reason alone, having children is for adults; when you are young and immature, you don't have the patience. That's normal to be young, immature, and not in a committed relationship; but having kids under those circumstances is a recipe for disaster. I once read a recent study where 80% of foster kids who are mentored fail, or end up on drugs, become prostitutes, or end up dead. That is a very high percentage of failing our children. All I asked young people to think about is their own lives, as well as the kid's lives. In the late eighties, we wanted to try raising the kids in a more family friendly environment. We decided to move to the Poconos in Pennsylvania. That's where Ashley began her pre-school education. The Poconos was a good place to relocate in the northeastern part of Pennsylvania. We honeymooned there. It was a nice inexpensive place to raise a family back then. We commuted to New York for work; I worked nights and Loretta worked days. I was able to be with the kids daily and mom nightly. Ashley was two years old and the boys only had to walk a short distance to the bus stop. We lived in a nice friendly development. The summers were beautiful and the winters were brutal. The winters were so bad they allotted a certain amount of snow days for school closings. Many days I had to stay overnight in New York due to inclement weather in Pennsylvania. After a year of traveling, my wife decided to find work locally and spend more time with the kids. As the boys got older, needless to say, sports and girls were next on the calendar, and not in that order. Being very involved in their lives, and paying close attention to their behaviors, I would always want to be ready for any concern they may have. The last thing you want is for your kids to learn life in the streets or from other kids who know as little as they do. This is where the tire hit the road. They would ask Dad, or "Pop" as my sons would call me, "I like so and so", or "I want to play ball", or Pop this or Pop that. Are you ready to help them make a good decision? Could you tell them "I don't mind you playing ball, as long as you do your homework, or pass your grades"? Or "son, having a girlfriend, could you continue to progress in school and give a girlfriend the amount of attention she deserves"? Playing ball was fine, as long as they passed their grades or behaved in school. To tell a young man not to have a girlfriend is like telling a boy to eat hot coals. They will find a way to have a girlfriend by any means necessary. I realized that, so I would remind them the last thing you want is a baby while going to school. Fathers have to support their kids; young fathers have to drop out of school to find a job, get an apartment, maybe two jobs. You can't play ball only your whole life would be ruined. The mother and baby come first. Not you, sports, or other girls. I'm happy to say that it worked. The struggles of their parents and to not raise kids through hardship impressed upon their minds very effectively. I must admit, my mother gave us the opportunity to play football, basketball, and the like; as long as we behaved in school and passed our grades. This woman use to work at night, come home, rest a little, and get up and work a second job. Watching her do this everyday, I decided to try-out for the sport of my choice (basketball) to make the first cut, satisfy my qualifications, and then get a job to help her with my personal expenses. I couldn't allow myself to play a sport in good conscious, and not assist a woman who was giving her all to make sure we had a roof over our heads and food to eat. I just couldn't do it. Thinking of how my whole childhood was robbed by not having the opportunity of being a

*Cousins: Lanard, PJ, Terrance, and Devon*

normal kid, my older brother suffered the same way. Being fatherless really took its toll on all of us. I wanted our kids to never go through the major personal sacrifices that my brothers and sisters went through without that father figure at home. Therefore, as the boys did well in school and in their personal lives, they were able to participate in athletics. Now girl friends, that was a sticky issue. They have been told about the birds and the bees, also the flowers and the trees. In sports, you play, practice, and that is it. With girls, its phone calls (money to pay for extra phone calls), spending time with them after school without cutting class, buying things without a job, etc. The problem is how do you tell a young man that seeing a girl right now is off limits? That's almost impossible. Young people will always find a way to see each other under any and all circumstances. What to do? What worked for me was that I was very close to my mom, and didn't want to disappoint her. I took under consideration, thought about getting a lady pregnant. That would have killed her, as would dropping out of school to support her and the baby. Also, what I was told in my congregation was to abstain until marriage for the very reason of becoming a father too soon. It was very hard. I still had young lady friends, but was very responsible about sex and going to far. I learned to not get myself in a compromising position; if you're not going to follow through, it could be quite embarrassing. The next day in school, everybody will find out that nothing happened. I used to hear other guy's adventures and said to myself "Oh my God, that must have been incredible", of course if the story was true. We guys make things up you know. It gets worse in the summer, when the weather is nice and both of us are feeling good. Those are painful years I never want to repeat. I simply told my boys about getting young ladies pregnant, the responsibility it involved, and how your whole life would never be the same if you become a father too soon. I also told them that you could wait until marriage, and their mother would say, "I'm not raising your children". We also prayed a lot, something that is always good. Nothing and nobody kept me away from the girls, and I believed the same would be true with our boys. I believe what worked for us was a lot of love and constant reminders of doing the right thing. And last but not least, being there! Many people I've noticed, underestimate the environment. It is very hard for kids to grow up doing the right thing when everything around them is wrong. Drugs on every corner, shootings every night, gang violence, etc. Areas such as these only breed more criminals and more crime. At every cost, or by any means necessary, don't raise your beloved children around these conditions. As parents, it is your job to raise them and give them the best opportunity possible to succeed. If you own a home, and your neighborhood has gone south, so should you and your family. Don't let your family be the sacrificial lambs. You will never forgive yourself. As a family head, be it a man or woman, it is your job to give your children the best opportunity possible to achieve in life. Do whatever it takes. Our boys played sports. Lanard played basketball, and Terrance played football and basketball. Terrance, our baby son, was the biggest of my sons. He also had to go through many test in regards to his patience. Many kids would try him, to see if he would fight them if teased. The kids were taught to never start fights; if hit then tell your teacher, that's what they are there for. I also told them if daddy finds out that you started a fight, then you had to come home and deal with pop. By then the ten- month rule of discipline was a struggle. It would be a little ridiculous to try to be a 6'10 son with muscles everywhere if I didn't start disciplining early. The oldest didn't have to assume any other position of taking any extra responsibilities because pop was home. All he had to do was grow up normal. He played high school ball in both the Poconos and New York. He graduated on time and went to college at his moms urging. In fact, she was the college advocate for all three of her kids. They all went right out of high school to college, without a break in between, to keep the flow going. That proved to be a good idea; it of course was struggle but well worth it. Keep in mind parents "our children didn't ask to come in this world, we chose to have unprotected sex and bring them here", be it responsibly or not, that was our choice. My mother took part in making seven children; she understood the responsibility that went into having seven children. When our father didn't feel the same responsibility for his six children that he participated in producing, he chose not to do what was necessary to raise us. No one, not my mother or anyone or anything, should have taken away his responsibility to help raise his kids. And I told him so. I simply said, "Pop, I'm married and have three children as you know, and there is no excuse for me, you, or any other man or woman, to not participate in the raising of their children. No excuses whatsoever. Besides, my grandfather, his father, was there for him up until he died. Young ladies, God gave you the most important thing to the average man aside from food and water or life itself. And that's the femininity and all that goes with it. Make a man appreciate it. Qualify yourself to not be just another pretty face, but a qualified woman. Learn how to cook (men too), clean, handle a home, and learn how to pay bills. If you are home with mom, learn from her. Boys are not going anywhere, learn to love and rely on yourself. Don't fall for that "you need a man" to validate yourself. A man loves a confident, secure woman that has a backbone. Just by being a woman, you will automatically attract a man. Let him know clearly that I'm worth a good, hard working, honest man. Let him know that one act of cheating, physical abuse, or mental abuse is either go to counseling or that's it. It's over; neither you nor he has any business touching each other unless it's a touch of passion or love. Love yourselves! If you respect yourself, he will have no choice but to love you as well. It is a god-given privilege to have a good mate; that's what men and women want. Ladies, when it comes to children, guess who was chosen to carry and bare the responsibility of delivering the child. What does that mean? It means that it wouldn't hurt to really know the man you may want to have children with. Know his family, control your sexual behavior, let men know that I don't want any children with an irresponsible man. If I get pregnant, you must be ready to be a father. When a woman stands up for herself, the man has no choice but to respect her. Young ladies, it's not that hard. That way abortions are not an option; unwanted children will not be an option. You have every bit of control of your lives. Don't let any man tell you differently. Every turn you make when it comes to parenting, you should be in a committed relationship like a marriage. You and your children deserve that commitment. I consider having children as a privilege and a gift from God. When it comes to a daughter, that is off the charts. What man doesn't want to spoil their little girl? Miss Ashley was a shy, quiet little girl. At four, like her brothers, she started pre-school in the Poconos. She never said much, her teacher thought she couldn't speak. I would drop her off and she would start crying. I had to stay with her way after school started so she wouldn't cry. Once she had gotten over her shyness, the young lady progressed well. Always good, no complaints about her behavior. Like her two aunts (my sisters), and her three aunts (her mother's sisters), I treated them as well as Ashley, like young princesses. Her mother was my queen; people would never confuse the two. While going to school in Pennsylvania, there was a pedophile attempting to grab kids from their bus stops. Her brothers would wait for her after school and I would take her to the bus stop when I could in the mornings. We moved back to New York temporarily for a couple of years. The boys graduated high school in Long Island while Ashley still was in grade school. The oldest did one year of college in Long Island and went to college in North Carolina. To pack him up at nineteen and put him on a bus was one of the hardest things to do as a parent. But we did it. As his two younger siblings continued to do well in New York, Lanard went to Charlotte North Carolina and attended two universities. He received his bachelor's degree in Political Science at the University of North Carolina at Charlotte. Going to Charlotte worked out well for him. My parents and older brother were born there, and he had plenty of relatives to assist him at every turn. North Carolina is a great state, and has plenty of great colleges there. To be a father requires a level of responsibility. You must be in touch with what to expect from your kids. Your advantage is you were once their ages. That's the prime reason to being an adult before having children. You can draw on your own personal experiences. When growing up, mom used to use every ounce of creative energy to raise us drawing on her experience of raising two of my uncles due to the lost of her parents at a young age. She had experience of how to deal with male problems and issues when it came to her five sons. She knew each one of her children, she knew how to reason, discipline, and direct each of us. She use to say, "Theodore, each one of you had your own distinctive kick when I was carrying you. Mom had to be convincing and persuasive, and when that didn't work, she had to be forceful. She was never afraid of us. I see her now, reaching up and hitting me upside my head when I

didn't get it. Being ready to guide them as needed, whenever mom needed male intervention, there were male members of the congregation to help. Mom taught us communication when she allowed us to go to parties or visit friends, be it on foot or by car. She would say, "Call me when you get there". When the boys left home, I told them I don't care if you were in China, Sundays was a day of mandatory communication during the week. Sundays was a must! It's nothing like hearing their voices just to know that they are all right. Some people may say that's a bit much, and I hear that. "You baby your kids". My response, "You do what works". And ladies and gentleman, to this day it's still working. I can't tell you the phone calls or cards that I have received from my boys over the years, or what they have told me. I'm embarrassed to admit when I start reading them, I never finish. Tears come to my eyes, the joy and appreciation. When my daughter was nine, accompanying her to school was a no no. In New York, her school wasn't too far from the house, but dad found a way to do it. Her teachers used to get a kick out of her wanting her independence while dad was being overly protective. The women teachers loved it; Ashley hated it. We relocated again in New York, and Ashley's junior high school was out of walking distance. I asked Terrance to assist in her travels to her new junior high school. He did, and she again was on her way. Speaking of Terrance, junior high went well. In high school, he decided that he had to be Mr. Personality, the charmer. Everywhere he went, his height was a factor. I didn't want him to get a pass because of it. I wanted him to work as hard as everyone else and to earn his stripes, which he did. It's nice to get attention everywhere you go, that's a plus, but you must keep your feet on the ground at all times. Their mother and I wanted them to always stay grounded and keep their senses. One of the more touching memories I had with anyone of my kids was at Terrance's graduation from high school. During the ceremony, he looked over and saw one of his classmates who was supposed to graduate with him but didn't. He remembered the value of working hard and getting to school on time. He walked over to his mother and me and said "Thank you dad for everything". He was helped to step it up a notch, to not waste one year of your life repeating a grade. Keep in mind young folks that a year of life you cannot get back; that year lost in school is gone. Terrance and I worked hard to make that happen; study, take school seriously, to be publicly educated is a privilege. Speaking of our great public school system, I never had a pre-school education but was able to become a hardworking good citizen in my country. I would like to advocate for young men and women, as well as our government and local state municipalities, to see the value of teaching young men and women to be responsible parents. How many more children do we as a nation have to see have more children before we act. When I was growing up, we were taught not to use drugs or even the pitfalls of cigarettes. It would be an advantage to start teaching our youth about being responsible fathers and mothers, what it takes to be good parents, to make them fully aware of the life long responsibility. I believe it should be part of their required courses. I'm sure it would benefit a great number of teenagers to think twice. While writing this book, I saw the pain in the face of the President of the United States while speaking about coming up without a father. Only someone that ever lived it can feel that pain. I mention my father to my older brother and it changes his whole thinking process; he stares into space reliving the horror of being a father figure and an adolescent at the same time. I want our experience of overcoming such a struggle to help other kids to believe they can make it too. But by the same token, they can just as easily fail. Kids have to rely on talk shows like Maury Povich, Tyra Banks, or court shows like Judge Hatchett (who is an excellent person who gets directly involved with troubled kids). Geraldo Rivera also back in the day had shows about troubled youth. The one and only Oprah Winfrey put her money were her mouth was, as did many others. When my daughter was thirteen, I had her to watch Maury Povich; he showed thirteen-year-old girls having babies, leaving home and becoming young prostitutes, talking back to their parents and disrespecting them. I simply told her "Honey, this is what your life could be if mom and dad didn't work so hard to give you kids everything material as possible, but mostly love and our time". I want to credit Maury Povich for the years of showing and exposing the pitfalls of our youth. Upon my daughters graduation party from high school, she hugged me and said "Dad, thanks for asking me to watch Maury Povich, it was good to see what my life could have been without you and moms love and sacrifice". So again, thank you Mr. Povich, Judge Mathis, and Judge David Young, who also administers DNA test to identify the fathers of these innocent children. Mr. Mathis reminds kids of his troubles as a teen, and once again, the mother helped him get it right. He is a perfect role model for all young men, both black and white. He also gives seminars and lectures to help troubled young men. Thank you Mr. Mathis, only if young men and women knew the lives they destroy by having children irresponsibly, they would think twice. Nothing I can say can replace the joy I would get when my wife and I would pull up in the drive-way, and I would see my daughter peeking through the blinds waiting for daddy to come home every night and take her to the local candy store to look at the latest teen magazines or just go driving and get candy. There is nothing like daddy's little girl. Terrance was finishing up high school and getting ready to graduate and start college. He was doing well enough to play basketball. He was growing quite well. At 6'8, I told him "Terrance, you know the routine. Basketball is a luxury and privilege, but good grades are a must"! He, like his older brother, played for their high school. I'll never forget that night, mom and I were sitting and talking while watching TV when we heard a knock at the door. Two of Terrance's team members were bringing him in to sit down. He had just snapped his ankle in three places during a Slam Dunk contest. Nothings guaranteed, at 6'10 an NBA career is possible. The lesson, what if he didn't have passing grades? What if he totally depended on playing basketball and forgot about an alternative to basketball? Some young people totally lose focus and turn to a dangerous path of life without a mom or dad to say, "Son, it's going to be alright. Son, your God given height will bless you in other ways". I certainly couldn't tell him that if I wasn't there. I couldn't tell him that if I was out doing my thing and said later for my kids, let mom handle that. By the grace of God, I was there to look him in the eye and say, "Son, mom and dad are here for you". It was a stinging lost for him. He'll never know some parents live through their kids. I wanted to play, so let me push him to play. Ladies and gentleman, basketball would have never come up if either of my sons didn't bring it up. They were raised to make their own lives with the help of both parents. After graduating high school with offers all over the country to play ball, he chose to play in California. His ankle was never the same, but we supported him and was there for him every step of the way. While Terrance was in California, Lanard was in

North Carolina getting his bachelors degree. Every so often, you have to pinch yourself and say, "Good guys do finish first if you keep trying". My next question was "How do you be there for your daughter and not be overly protective"? To this day, I'm still trying to figure that out. That's a job but guess what, it must be done. Basically, when you raise kids to be honest, they will tell you. And yes, my daughter reminds me every time it gets too much for her. "Thank you dad, I can do it. I'm fine". I was the same way with my two younger sisters; they knew they had brothers who loved them and were there for them. I would like at this time to pause, although expected, the passing of a TV actress who many young men made it a point to have her poster on their wall, the lovely Farrah Fawcett. This day, while enjoying the lovely weather writing this book outside, I received word that she had just died. Anyone's passing is a tragedy, but this one is extremely personal. Not only have I seen too many friends who suffered a premature death due to cancer, but my beloved mother and sister, to whom this book is dedicated to as well, suffered and died of cancer. Ms. Fawcett did an excellent acting job in "The Burning Bed" and in "Charlie's Angels" along with Kate Jackson and Jaclyn Smith; the mysterious Charlie was fun to listen to also. I wish Mr. Ryan O'Neil, and her son (who was still incarcerated at the time of her passing), and their families the very best. I feel their pain; I'm still suffering the lost of my mother and sister. On the same day, and at the same time of being notified of Ms. Fawcetts's death, I was taken totally by surprise of the passing of Mr. Michael Jackson. Here was a man, in fact the only man, who could arguably be compared to the hardest working man in show business, Mr. James Brown. James Brown was my musical favorite, but I enjoyed Frank Sinatra, the incomparable Sammy Davis Jr., Ella Fitzgerald, Liza Minelli, Diana Ross, The Temptations, well you get the picture. If I start with music and musicians, that would be a five hundred page book all to itself. But the passing of Michael Jackson was very disappointing. Here was a man God gave everything, talent, good looks, great family situation, a wonderful mother (who from what I've read, is a God fearing woman). She and her husband probably raised the most talented family in show business history. I can't imagine raising such a talented family without even more problems than they had. My prayers go out to "The Jackson" family as well. Watching another entertainment legend in his own right, Mr. Denzel Washington, host a show some years ago in reference to a situation involving Michael Jackson, I believe he said, "If much is given, much is expected". Literally hundreds of millions of young people idolized Michael across the globe. That was a great opportunity to be a great example for them. Let's hope Michael lived up to such great expectations. With that said, Miss Ashley made her way through junior high school quite easily with little to no incidents. In high school, she and one of her cousin began going to a newly built school in which they both were the first graduating group who attended the school. She was fortunate enough to make the honor role three times while attending the school. She being the first granddaughter on my side to have accomplished this feat, we were very proud of her. Before graduating, she expressed an interest in work. So I took her to the local Wal-Mart,

*Mom and Ashley.*

and she couldn't complete the application process because she never worked before. So I helped her get a job at Burger King while attending her first year of college. My daughter was very interested in business; she wanted to be a Business Administration major, something that the economy single handedly killed in its tracts. Miss Ashley wanted to attend school in the south where her brother lived. Since she had much family living in that part of the country, she would have to travel south and seek out the school of her choice, then find work. By the time she did go south, she decided to work part-time at the local Wal-Mart while attending school. It seemed like it was just yesterday; here she is, my little princess talking about attending college. When we came up to the Poconos initially, she was only two years old. Now she's nineteen and talking about attending a southern college to complete her studies. The memories of having visitor come up to enjoy the comforts of the Poconos, while her mother would show the visitors around, I would baby-sit the kids. My daughter and her brothers would play with the other kids, but when I had enough, I would tell everybody to sit down and relax. My kids knew the drill and of course, the other kids didn't. I would say "Uncle Teddy is a little tired, relax and I would get you some ice cream". Most of the kids would get the message and some of the others wouldn't. I would say if you don't sit, I'll tell your mom and dad. For the most part, they would listen and cooperate. I would see kids in stores running wild and not listening in public. Our rule was discipline at home; have them sit down, gather themselves, and don't get carried away while playing. And when they refused, that's when those little legs got popped. They must understand that they must obey and sit down when told. The visiting parents realized that if you visit Uncle Teddy's house, you must sit down when asked just like Ashley and her brothers. It won't kill them to learn to sit every now and then. Teaching the kids takes time; you must be consistent. They must believe that you are serious. If not, the kids will walk all over you and embarrass you while out in public. The memories last forever. I would tell visiting kids that you must listen to Uncle Teddy; when my kids don't, I get those little legs. The worst punishment for a normal child is to make them sit down for a period of time. With all that energy, that drives them crazy, but at the same time in the long run, it teaches them or gets them use to developing self-control and improves their behavior. Give it a try. Ashley's graduation party was a family reunion. Her brothers came home, all of her relatives were able to attend, and she was totally surprised to see everyone show up. This was a young woman who played by the rules, stayed out of trouble, and gave the first eighteen and a half years of her life the best shot. There were plenty of reasons to do wrong. Her mother and father had plenty of issues between them; but she and her brothers were raised believing in God, and we tried to maintain a home that understood the benefits of putting family first along with love for each other. People were coming to her party as late as nine o'clock at night; it was some testimony of a really decent young lady.

*Ashley and the Twin Towers.*

# *The Challenge*

We just highlighted the first twenty-seven years of a father along with his wife, who were just as imperfect as the next couple, who had a chance to do the right or the wrong thing in life. I as a man love the women; like most men. I didn't have to follow my mother's example and instruction. I didn't have to listen to one of the brightest and hardest-working women ever to achieve your best efforts and not your worst. I didn't have to appreciate the beauty of one of Gods best creations. The woman, a person who deserves the man's utmost respect, must love themselves enough to not be hooked on drugs, commit crimes, and to jail. To reach for excellence, again the parent's involvement is important. Don't expect your kids to achieve when their surroundings are bad. It has been done, children can rise above the despair, but you are playing a game of Russian roulette with your children. We as women and men, girls and boys, should Stop, Look, and Listen. Look in the mirror and challenge yourself. Do I want to be a sideshow on TV or a success story in life; a person who people admire and look up to? Search your soul, develop the audacity of hope, and achieve your goals. First, you have to set goals to achieve goals. Don't let the sacrifice of so many before us go to waste. Being respectable is achievable; it has been done before. I've been very fortunate to think of others while being there for my kids. I've talked to many a young man and woman to go for your best instincts and don't be afraid to reach for the stars. A jail cell is not for humans, why put yourself in a situation like that because of a senseless crime. Again, fellas, if you love women, you won't find them behind bars. That was my theme to young men and women whenever I worked or spoke with young people who care to listen. While attending a seminar in the late 90's in New York City, I was privileged to run into the son of Black Enterprise Publisher Earl Graves.

We had a very nice conversation about life and goals. Our conversation went so well that he offered to do a story on my life. I was humbled by the offer to the point of never getting back to him. That offer made this ordinary father in his early forties continue to appreciate staying focused and doing the right thing. If my life story can help or benefit other mothers and fathers, then my mission was accomplished. We all should want to not forget where we came from and help others. Young men and women, this is considered a very exciting time. Young people are inspired around the world to be positive and optimistic. The world economy is effecting everyone but at the same time, look at it as a new beginning. Retool your skills; try different things. Search your souls for different talents. Don't forget the expression "necessity is the mother of invention". The economy won't stay bad forever. Recreate yourselves; look for a need in the world. Again, challenge yourself to get a better job, to complete your education, to seek higher education, to enter public service. I worked in public service for twenty-one years; make yourself necessary. God gave all of us a personal skill. Find yours and don't make excuses. Again, I give my older brother credit for thinking of me when he attempted to serve in the public service sector. He attempted, but never started. I went on to a twenty-year plus career. Life has many challenges, both good and bad. Say to yourself that the bad choices are not an option. A perfect example of struggle is the first family. Whatever your ideology, theirs was a struggle that took them to the highest public service position in this country. The President turned all of the negatives into positives. The First Lady lost her father, had a mother who kept her and her brother focused, and went to college. She became a hospital administrator in Chicago, and now The First Lady. After doing research for my daughter to look towards the medical field, I used the experience of the First Lady Michelle Obama as an example of what an intelligent and determined woman of color can do. Do not make excuses. That's easy, and needless to say, my little girl made the Dean's list her first year of school. A hero of mine is Spike Lee, along with Sylvester Stallone. Both are film writers, and both made their own careers. Oprah Winfrey and Martha Stewart are self-made women in a so-called man's world. Tyra Banks turned modeling into a television empire. I grew up watching Jack Lalane and his wife using household furniture to bring exercising into every home in the sixties. On TV today, Judge Mathis left prison and in fifteen years became a judge. That has to be a record for achievement. Maybe your niche is sports. Magic Johnson turned sports into philanthropy. He didn't forget where he came from and he reached back. The young Alicia Keys, one of the best songwriters and musicians in the business, did not forget about others. Before you can help others, you have to help yourself. You have to be a role model. None of the people I mentioned are perfect people, but they just applied themselves to be the best they can be. A good number of young people don't' think living by principles is necessary. They believe you can do whatever you want without having to think twice about the consequences of their actions. Keep in mind many of the laws we live by in this country are laws that were outlined in the bible. Being brought up strict; my mother reminded us and taught us principles from the bible. It's impossible to follow every principle perfectly but using its principles is a good measuring stick that can't hurt. There is good information in the bible on being a responsible parent, "If you don't work then you don't eat". A man should have one wife, and a wife should have one husband. A man should value and cherish a woman; a woman should respect her husband. Yes, those laws I grew up on and I tried to live by. I failed many times but picked myself up and kept trying. All I'm asking is that we keep trying. I'm still trying; it will never end. Another principle I tried to live by is helping others. In this book, there will be a number of young people I will highlight whose life experiences may be helpful to many of you. These are young people who I worked with, and encouraged them to have self-respect. Value your own lives; respect others, and make a good life for yourself. My children will highlight their personal experiences by telling how they kept their goals of making it to the finish line. Both their mother and I struggled from start to finish. While growing up, I read there is more joy in giving than there is in receiving. I use to laugh at that verse until I tried it. When I started, I couldn't stop.

Sharing my time and my experiences (I couldn't share money) is a feeling that cannot be duplicated. Just knowing that you helped someone is quite satisfying. With incredible people like, Mother Theresa, or princess Diana, these ladies gave time and energy to many causes which included Bill Gates, his wife Oprah Winfrey and Michael Jackson. Michael Jackson over his career, gave over three hundred million dollars to charity. I was told as a young man, "Teddy, you don't have to go to auto-mechanic school to be a good mechanic. You don't have to be rich to be rich in your soul". Life is a learning process, being a good person starts within and works its way out. Something that we all can achieve if we make it a way of life. Young men, treat every young lady as you want another young man to treat your sister. Young ladies, treat young men as you would want your brother treated. Each of us has a responsibility to ourselves and to others. To get respect you must give it. That is a good rule to live by. Although young, my wife was a woman who likes keeping her house clean. Cooking she could take or leave, but she was good at that too. I enjoyed working. I understood what I had to do as a father. Young men, are you ready for that role? There is plenty of eye candy for both of you, being in a relationship with children, are you ready to be with just one? A serious question that needs a serious answer. Think about all of the young kids that will grow up in this world not knowing who their father is. Why add to that number? Why Treat Children as, litter, Garbage, dropping one here, and one there, does the world need another fatherless or helpless child? Don't be part of the problem, be a part of the solution. The following are the latest statistics of fatherless children in the United States and young women who are having children out of wedlock: 83.1% of single parents are mothers and 71% of pregnant teens are from fatherless households. These statistics are chilling, but they could be avoided. The number of children in foster homes in the United States is approximately 500,000. The percentage of children that grow up without an identity and turn to prostitution or become victims of crimes in the U.S. is 33%. Is that what you want to be a part of? Think about it, this is very serious stuff. One of the hardest programs on TV to watch are programs that feature fatherless children. Many times, it's the fathers who are blamed for this problem and rightfully so. But what part does the woman play in this out of control problem? A major part! Not only can a woman deny a man complete access or make a man use contraception, but choose to not have him touch you at all. This strength on your part not only protects you, but it eliminates the responsibility of raising children by yourself. Just think of a child growing up not knowing who their father is? Let's examine a few examples of what I mean. One program had a beautiful couple on TV where the woman had the man paying child support for years. She had him thinking the child was his but they ended up taking a DNA test at the man's request. The results concluded that the child was not his and the mother was aware of this but lied to him because he made the most money between the two men that she was sleeping with. Another example, a woman forced her mother to find out who her father was by having all of the men that she had intercourse with take a DNA test. There are programs like this were three or four men are taking DNA test and still none of them are the father. These are women in their thirties and forties. These people are devastated. Their lives are affected forever. There are millions of examples of young men and women going to their graves not having a clue as to who their father is. I was once young and excited about being with a young lady, but the thought of making a baby and telling my mother would have torn her apart. My mom had five sons who had to think and be mindful of such a possibility. This was before DNA test were thought of. I got to the point where the only reason it did not happen to me was because of disappointing my mother. Don't forget, I was brought up very religious. I challenge myself to not make a baby before my time. Fellas, at seventeen I did the unthinkable. A high school lady friend and I planned to cut school and go to her house. We got there and watched a little TV. She went upstairs to get ready but I'm downstairs going crazy trying to figure out how to get out of this situation knowing mom would kill me if she found out. Fellas, at that moment I wish I had gone to Coney Island instead. When I got the call, I went upstairs, I ask, you how do you change direction in midstream where one of the loveliest ladies in your school is laying under a sheet in her birthday suit. It was show time and guess what? The next day I was the laughing stock at school. It seemed that the whole senior lunch period looked at me as if I was from Mars. Needless to say, she stopped talking to me. This same situation happened to me not once but twice. The first time it happened in junior high school, a young lady and I were in my bedroom; we go under my covers and I faked as if I went to sleep. I tried to get her to my house for months. Fighting the urge to want was not easy for me either. There were incidents when I would walk the lady friend of mine to her front door and not go in when invited knowing anything could happen beyond those doors. The most powerful persons on this earth are women, their influence and sex appeal is unmatched. Trust me. We men have to respect their God given prowess. Think about it, how many men have four or five children from four or five different women? Millions of us I'm told. When you make a child out of wedlock or a non-relationship, both the man and woman wish that they never met. Think about that, one of the best acts in life is regretted just because

*Dad, Grandma, and Lanard. This book is*
*dedicated to the late Gladys Russell*

you did it the wrong way. I can't imagine regretting that I made love to the mother of my child or children. That must be the worse feeling in the world. It's a shame to say more money is spent on prisons, then housing for unloved children, who were the victims of parents not taking their responsibility seriously. The State or Federal Government should not do our jobs as parents. This is a global problem and it starts at home, and early at that. Speaking of early teaching of our children, while watching excerpts of the Michael Jackson memorial, it was hard to watch many parts of it because it was too sad. When his daughter couldn't finish memorializing her father, it killed me. That little girl at twelve years old no longer has a father to help raise her. Ladies and gentleman, that's sad. What his daughter is going through, millions of young boys and girls are in that same situation without the family support that she will get for the rest of her life. Find that tape and look at the pain that was evident on her little face. Don't do that to our kids fathers, don't do it! At eleven or twelve years old, her little heart will be heavy forever. If you are nowhere in sight for your children, what is the difference between not being there or being dead? Fellas, I'm the last person to say don't interact with girls, being intimate is a decision that I can't make for anybody, but don't let our children suffer like that. At the age of twenty-one, I decided to risk my life along with two sisters by racing another member of my congregation. Two cars trying to out do each other down New York's Belt Parkway, doing speeds of ninety miles per hour and just taking life for granted. As a young man, my elevator did not always reach the top floor. The other driver baited me into a race. I had a custom-made sports car so everyone wanted to race me. I lost control, ripped the back of my car, to the point, where you could see the street from the front seat of my car because the back seat and the trunk were missing. I had hit a lamp pole and missed the gas tank by inches. We could have had an explosion that night. A passenger had to go to the hospital due to a concussion. The young ladies father told me if I didn't like you much, I would hit you in the jaw. To be alive and write this book makes me feel privileged and grateful. After such an experience, I learned my lesson. After it was clear that I was not injured, mom let me have it. I was punished. A grown man being punished for stupidity. I admit it; there was no reason for that to happen. I didn't make any excuses; I lost a respected position in my congregation, and almost killed five people for lack of maturity. My point, some of us survive stupidity, and some of us don't. I never repeated this act again. That was my challenge, to have survived such an accident and nobody was killed in the process or even seriously hurt. We were all very fortunate. Some weeks later, I had to return to the car to get something out of the glove compartment. I looked at the car in disbelief. To this day, I cannot imagine how all five of us survived. A very hard lesson to forget needless to say. My challenge at twenty-one was to not under any circumstance, ever put my life or anybody else's life in jeopardy by racing at that speed again. I challenged myself to not repeat the same serious mistakes again. Therefore, my two major challenges were to not have a child without being in a serious and committed relationship, and not risk the life of myself or anybody else by being reckless behind the wheel. My other challenges were to not repeat my father's mistake of abandoning

*The late Aunt Chantel, Grandpa, and cousin Maurice Butler*

my children under any circumstances. So young men and women, don't be afraid to challenge yourself.

I spoke earlier of giving back. After the kids were grown and on their own, I began working in retail. You meet many young folks just out of school trying to decide where to go to college or work. It felt good to help them decide their futures. Being a young adult, you have mom and dad issues, boyfriend and girlfriend issues, wanting to be independent, etc. How do you be there and assist them? Well, I asked them "how are you doing in school"? And "what do you want to do when you complete school"? Then I just listen to what they have to say. That is how I started with my quest to help young adults begin their path. Being a good listener usually begins with a smooth transition to helping young adults open up to you and focus on their futures. That technique I learned through the bible teachings as a young adult myself. One of the books I studied was called "Be a good listener". People, know when you are genuinely interested in listening and assisting them (like the popular expression "If you want the truth, ask a child". They will tell you the truth, lying is something they have to learned). Once Trust is established, then the listening of the young adults begins. The way I established credibility with many young adults was to tell them about my decisions made while I was their age, and also helping to raise my children when they were their age. I would tell them of my challenges, how my mother raised seven children from the early sixties to the late seventies. I would tell them you are going to make many mistakes but there are some mistakes you could avoid altogether, and those are the serious ones. At a certain age, you don't have to hit yourself in the hand with a hammer to know that it will be painful. I would tell them some decisions you make, there is no turning back from them. For example, serious crimes will land you in jail. Once you have felonies against you, that will impact your life forever. Sometimes young men have more difficulty listening than young women; we men like a challenge and I tell them don't challenge me, challenge yourself. You are the future; I will soon be the past. Make a difference, be an example and always look at yourself as a big brother leading the way for a younger sibling. Put in your mind that failure is not an option. I had the privilege to work with two young ladies who really appreciated the way I treated them and cared for them like my own daughters.

*The Graduate! Bachloer of arts from UNC Charlotte. Lanard was the first grandchild to graduate with a degree from college on both sides of his family.*

# Crystal and Shameka: Their stories

One of my most gratifying experiences in being a father is reaching out to young people. I found that most young men I spoke to under twenty years old make sex very important in their lives. That's very normal but it must be in moderation. When asked to balance their outlook or goals, they get offended. On the other hand, young ladies under twenty may feel the same way but they at least listen to why they should be cautious and protect their temple (body). They should cherish their body and not make it available for the sake of sex. I was able to meet and work with two such ladies. They both were well raised and smart young women. They, like their male counterparts, liked the attention of young men but they listed and took many words of wisdom to heart. I became their adopted uncle so to speak. These young ladies called and sent me text messages on Father's Day along with my own three children. Both families were very appreciative of the support and fatherly advice I gave them. They also kept me up to date with the new changes in young America, which I appreciated. The friendships continue to this day. They both are progressing well as young twenty something year old women. The joy of giving your time and advice to those who appreciate it is unmatched. It truly was worth my time. Probably one of the greatest joys in life is to see your children grow up and go their separate way to do well. When their father asked them to contribute to this book their personal experiences, I wasn't sure that they would agree to it. Such a project could get very personal. To my pleasant surprise, they agreed with the understanding that their personal experience just might help someone else. If our experience can make a father think twice about abandoning a mother and child, then this book and the hours put into writing it was worth it. All three of my busy children took time out of their schedules to send me their personal stories of attempting to keep their eyes on the goal of living a full and responsible life. Each one of them was contacted and asked to send me a summarization of whatever they want to contribute. I explained that I gave a basic summary of their grandmother and grandfather, my youth, their birth experiences, and their school years. I will start with my oldest and work my way to my youngest. Lanard when asked, "What kept you focused in school"? He said competitiveness and determination channeled his energies to excel in all subjects. Of course you are better at some subjects than others and according to him, his best subjects were English, writing, reading, and history. When I would pick him up from pre-school, over a period of three to four months one of his teachers asked me if his mother and I would consider having him begin first grade studies. He was an over achiever and was getting bored with pre-school and kindergarten activities. After discussing it with his mother, we agreed. As he progressed further in school, he said he challenged himself to do better and better. As he matured, he came to terms with the fact that math and science were the subjects that he needed the most improvement in. Ultimately, he said that he wanted to make his mother and father proud. I must admit that those were the best words a parent can ever hear from their own children. When it came to maintaining his grades, I wanted to know how did he not mix with the wrong kids, and of course how was he able not to have children young. Having the opportunity of going to school with kids of different backgrounds, he associated with men and women of a certain level of sophistication and who had goals and similar values. Terrance was more of a practical joker. While coming up, he had fun in school but did what he had to do to get through grade school. Like his older brother, he went to pre-school and did well. Setting goals as a young man, he realized that he was growing physically at an alarming speed. He said with good grades and knowing how he was raised, he would be able to play sports such as football and basketball. With such God given height, this helped him stay focused and set goals. Not excelling in school was considered a failure. Terrance liked to entertain lady friends but he realized the possibility of having children too early. The fear of catching and STD was a major factor. Realizing how having a child prior to him being ready would set him back too far. Some of his friends and family members had children before they were ready and that made him understand the magnitude of becoming a father. Ashley, my baby, quietly became a steady and focused student. When asked how she avoided repeating any grades, she stated that she took school very serious and followed the examples that her brothers set before her. All three of them understood that a year lost is a year wasted. That is one year you can't get back. Being twenty-two on her next birthday, I asked the question of how she avoided pregnancy and the drama that can go along with an early or unwanted pregnancy. She of course credited her mother for waiting until she was stable and married. She also saw the trouble that other young ladies were going through that were forced to become mothers prematurely. Her goals were to go to college and be in a stable relationship. I remind you about me having her watch Maury Povich at age thirteen. Once again, I want to thank my kids for their contribution, besides this whole project is about them. Although all three of our kids are grown, we're very involved in their lives. With this bad economy, it made us even closer. Careers have to be revisited; jobs that were profitable three or four years ago are not anymore. To be there and help make changes or suggestions is also important with your family. When the kids were young, we were back and forth between two states and relied heavily on family and friends to navigate the best possible life for them. Guess what, they responded and rose to the occasion. While writing this book, I focused on a particular TV program, "Black in America 2". This show focused on black family's struggles in the United States and Africa. The show highlights strong determined men and women giving back to their communities, reaching back to help young children, advocating that education can only help young people of all backgrounds. I want to thank CNN for having programs like "Heroes", which highlights regular people for the good deeds they do. In addition, shows such as "Latino in America" help focus people of color to not give up on yourselves. Thanks to Ms. Solidad O'Brien for doing such a wonderful job in her broadcasting. While this book is mainly speaking to young men and women about being responsible parents, another important topic I want to visit is HIV and AIDS. This is a major concern for young people, as well as older individuals. This topic requires an abundance of research and will be addressed at a later time. At this time young men and women, this book will bring forward five scenarios and circumstances that may interest and help young people overcome.

# Jackie's Story

Jackie, fourteen years old, is the oldest of three. She has two younger brothers who depend on her leadership. Her mother works two jobs to make ends meet. Jackie is starting to pay attention to her looks, as are the young boys. The mother must depend on Jackie's leadership and maturity, Jackie is responsible for leaving school on time and picking up both of her brothers from their bus stops. She enjoys the attention from the young boys and wants to stay after school to watch the boys play basketball or hang out with her girlfriends. She is pressured by the boys to stay after school and let the brothers venture home on their own. What should she do? Should she give in to peer pressure or follow her mother's instructions to look out for her brothers? Many young women face the same decisions. When their mothers have to fill the role as the father, the oldest must be there for their siblings. Their lives are restricted, but is that a bad thing? Is this a simple case of turning lemons into lemonade? Jackie has plenty of time for boys. When young teens are not careful, unplanned children can easily result. Jackie would benefit more from taking her mother's advice and helping out with her brothers. Jackie is very fortunate that she has a mother who cares and provides for her. She can take her time, equip herself with a college education, and be selective about who she involves in her life. "Will he be a man who loves me"? "Is he focused on finishing school"? What happens if I get pregnant, will he be there"? Young women bare the burden of the child if the man leaves. This is the perfect time for Jackie's mother to help her with her own ambitions and ask does she want to work as hard as she does. If you involve yourself with the wrong man, this is how you could end up. Jackie is determined to not fall prey to her temptations and listens to her mother's advice. Jackie is becoming more popular with the boys and her girlfriends are asking her to re-think her resistance to hanging out with them after school and meeting some of the boys. Her mother notices that Jackie was late picking up her brothers; they had to stay at their bus stops an extra twenty-five minutes, which resulted in all of the drop-offs being late. Because of this, the bus drivers reported this back to the school. Jackie's mother received word of this but chose not to confront her about it. It happened again the following week and because of this, Jackie's mother decided to talk to her about it. Jackie's mother knew the problem, but wanted to explain to Jackie that her studies and her two young brothers need her full cooperation. Jackie was honest with her mother and told her that she wants a boyfriend and that her friends are pressuring her to not pass up one of the star athletes at school. Her mother said she understands and asked to meet him. She asked Jackie whether or not she is being pressured to have sex by this boy. Jackie hesitated and said yes. She asked Jackie if she wanted to sleep with him, which Jackie replied yes. She said "Honey, that's normal but much too early". She asked Jackie to invite him over for dinner Friday night so they can discuss it. The mother asked Jackie not to mention the topic beforehand and that it will be discussed at the dinner table. They both agreed and Friday arrives. The mother helps Jackie prepare his favorite dish. She reminds her daughter about women having to cook, work, and take care of the kids. Her suitor arrives. When the bell rings, the mother says it would be nice if her brought flowers. Jackie answers the door, and Gregory comes in. They greet each other, Gregory is dressed very nicely but he does not have any flowers. Jackie welcomes him to the kitchen and he meets her mother. Gregory greets her mother, which she does in return. Jackie's mother informs them that dinner is almost ready and that they can have a seat in the living room. Jackie calls for her two brothers to come downstairs and she introduces them to Gregory. Gregory jokes that these are the two that keeps her away from him, which Jackie replies "Right"! Jackie's mother instructs everyone to wash their hands and have a seat at the dinner table. Jackie goes to help her mother with bringing the food to the dinner table but Gregory asks to help. Once everybody is seated, Gregory is asked to bless the food. Puzzled, Gregory confesses that he's never said grace before and does not know what to say. Jackie's mother responds by telling him to say whatever is in his heart. He thanks God for life, the food, and that he is liked by Jackie's mother. She thanks Gregory for such a heart-felt prayer, but she notices that he is very nervous. She asks Gregory how is his mother. Gregory responds that she is not good because she is in prison. She asks who is raising Gregory while his mother is incarcerated, and he replies his grandmother. When asked about his father, Gregory replies that he hardly sees his father because he works all day just like Jackie's mother. Surprised, she asks Gregory how does he know she works all day, and he says Jackie told him. She ask Gregory his age, which he replies sixteen and a half, and how well is he doing in school. Gregory's reply is that he does well enough in school to play basketball. During the conversation, Gregory's cell phone rings. He excuses himself from the table and answers it. It's Gregory's father and Gregory lets him know that he is having dinner with Jackie's family and that he'll be home late. Gregory let's her know that his father called to checkup on him and that he thanked her for having Gregory over for dinner. She asks Gregory how far does he live from here, which he replies eight blocks. She then asks him how does he feel about Jackie. Gregory states that he likes Jackie very much and that he gets a little jealous of her brothers because of the attention and responsibilities that she has towards them. Jackie's mother understood where he was coming from and extended an invitation for Gregory to give her a call anytime that he needs a person to talk to about school, or anything else for that matter. She goes on to say that Jackie has very big plans for her life, and at this time having children at a young age does not fit into those plans. She goes on to say that at both of their ages, they should be focused on building their characters, their grades in school, and focusing on their futures. Having a child can be a burden on their futures at this time and could also have a negative effect on their feelings toward each other. Getting caught up in passion and not using protection could result in an unplanned child and trouble. Jackie is quiet, and her mother asks why. Jackie replies by thanking her for this conversation and how she is thankful that her mother keeps her busy and focused and how she does not want any unplanned babies to affect her chances of college. She says that Gregory does not want children early either, which he strongly agrees. Gregory mentions a teammate of his that is seventeen and has to work after school to support his son because his parents can't afford to do it themselves. Dinner is over and Jackie asks Gregory to help her clean up the dishes. Gregory helps her out and compliments Jackie's mother for such wonderful food. She accepts his compliment and says that she will go upstairs to get some rest prior to her having to work later on that night. She tells Gregory to stay focused on his goals and dreams. Gregory stays a little longer and watches TV with Jackie and her brothers. Gregory mentions to Jackie that this evening with her mother made him miss his mother. Jackie asks him whatever happened to his mother. Gregory gives her an uncomfortable stare and replies, "I need a little time to let this night pass, your mom really made me think about a lot of things". Jackie interrupts and tells her brothers that it is getting late and that it is time for them to get ready for bed. She asks Gregory to continue his story. Gregory goes on to say that he really had a good time tonight and that he can't wait until his next visit to Jackie's home. He said that he felt bad to come off so selfish to her mother for wanting to spend more time with her. He says that most likely Jackie and her mother have had talks about him, and Jackie confirms that. Jackie tells Gregory that she and her mother have a wonderful relationship and talk about everything. Right then Jackie's mother calls out from upstairs letting her know that it is time for Jackie to get ready for bed also. Gregory says that is his sign to get ready to leave and thanks Jackie for such a wonderful night.

This was an illustration of two young people who were very interested in each other but chose to respect themselves and each other. Jackie could have easily created problems by not listening to her mother and take the selfish route by thinking of her own personal wants and desires. The mother noticed her daughter's behavioral changes and she acted on it. She obviously taught her from an early age to respect her motherly authority, to even think twice before doing what her heart wanted. As parents, you must keep your eyes and ears open to your children's changes of behavior, and young people must listen to their parents. Boyfriends or girlfriends are great, but you must not engage in sex before the time is right, otherwise you could regret your actions forever. I don't have to write every single detail, all you have to do is turn on your TV to find that. The purpose of sharing these stories is to help young people to look at another way of doing things. The key to avoiding an auto accident, drug overdose, or dropping out of school is to look ahead to the consequences. It's called preventive measures of disaster. I remind you of what kept me from going after every pretty girl I liked sexually; it was getting a woman pregnant and disappointing my mother, and becoming a father too soon. I want all young people to think of the consequences before they act. I came up very religious, but there were times when I said that God will forgive me, but my mother may not.

# Rodney's Story

This is a story about a young man named Rodney, a young man who was born out of wedlock to his parents both of whom raised him while not together. They strongly urged Rodney not to repeat their mistake of having a child while he was young, but he made the same mistake. Rodney's parents were two middle class, college educated young adults who were good friends, not in a relationship, but were sexually active and did not believe in abortions. In their day, AIDS and HIV was not an issue. His mother is a Pediatrician and his father is a Hospital Administrator. They met in college while she was a sophomore, and he was senior. They decided to bring him in the world and raise him, despite going in two different directions in their lives. After finding out his past, Rodney never understood why his parents did not stay together. It troubled him and at age sixteen, he started to question why he could not have a child or two before marriage. His girlfriend was a very beautiful young woman. She too was raised by parents out of wedlock, she had a lot in common with Rodney, so he felt there was no issue if he was to have children with her. Rodney likes his stepfather, but he really wishes that his biologic parents had stayed together. His girlfriend, Renee, is a seventeen-year-old track runner who has aspirations to go to law school. Rodney wants to study chemistry, and is a member of the track team. They both hoped to go to Ivy League colleges one day and they both did realize that pregnancy is not on the radar right now. If they were to have unprotected sex, they would be extremely careful. Renee's mother and stepfather owned a fast food chain, and she has an older sister and one younger brother. Her sister is a junior at Columbia University majoring in business, and her brother is fifteen in high school. While at a track meet at another school, Rodney and Renee's team had to stay overnight due to inclement weather. They were put up in a hotel near their meet. Before this track meet, they both had a kissy feely relationship, but this time it went a lot further. The team won big and Renee was the star of the day. She set a high school record in the 100-meter dash for her conference. The team was allowed to party since they had such an impressive win and they were staying overnight. All the kids' parents were notified of the layover. Renee was very excited about her accomplishment and so was Rodney. They were urged by their teammates to celebrate, but the coaches suggested that everybody go to bed due to a long trip the following day. They both laughed off the suggestion, and Rodney's roommate Jeff suggested that he would switch with Renee and stay in her room while Renee stays in their room. Jeff was very adamant about this mainly because he was very interested in Renee's roommate. Renee's roommate, Sarah, said that usually the coaches are asleep by 1 AM, so at this time they can do the room switch. Rodney was really feeling the pressure to go along with this, but he calls Renee on her cell phone. Renee answers it, and Rodney asks her if she wants to go along with this. Renee tells him yes but she does not have any condoms with her. Rodney does not have any either, but he is sure that Jeff has plenty and will ask him for some. 1 AM comes, and Sarah tells Renee that she is going to go to Rodney's room and Rodney will come to theirs. She says she'll be back not to long after 3 AM that way nobody gets suspicious. Meanwhile, Rodney asks Jeff for condoms but Jeff tells him that he only has two and may need them both. Jeff tells him to just go over to Renee's room and he'll see about getting him some. There is a knock at their door, Rodney answers and sees Sarah. Sarah excitingly tells him that Renee is waiting for him. Rodney grabs his overnight bag, which includes a towel, washcloth, underclothes, but no condoms. "I'll see you about 5 AM before the coaches wake up," Rodney tells Jeff. "Sure thing man, have fun" is Jeff's reply. On the way to Renee's room, Rodney is starting to have second thoughts about the plans. He does not feel ready for this but if he does not go through with the plans, he is afraid what everybody at school will say. Meanwhile, Renee is having the same thoughts. She too feels as if she is not ready but if Rodney is ready, then she can't say no. She did not know what the kids at school would say about her. A few minutes go by and Rodney knocks at Renee's door. Renee is so scared that she does not answer the door. Rodney knocks again and asks if she is sleep. Renee thinks to herself that may be just the excuse she needs to not go through with being intimate, the fact that she was sleep and Rodney woke her up. She opens the door for Rodney while faking a stretch and yawning. She asks him what time is it. Rodney reluctantly says it's a little after 2 AM. He does not want to mention that it took him a long time because he was trying to see if anybody else had condoms. Renee mentions that she fell asleep because her body is aching. Rodney's eyes light up and responds "Really"? Renee asks him what were Jeff and Sarah doing when he left. Rodney tells her that Jeff was already in bed when Sarah got over there, and that Sarah looked like she was ready to jump right in. Renee turns and looks at the TV thinking to herself that Rodney may have said that just to convince her not to back down. Rodney in the meanwhile is feeling uneasy thinking that he suggested to Renee that they have sex even though he does not have a condom and they already discussed that there would not be sex without protection. Renee tells Rodney that it's late, by the way are you hungry? Rodney replies that he is, and Renee feels a sigh of relief but also feels a little insulted that Rodney has not made an attempt to become intimate with her. Their motel was next to a 24-hour restaurant that delivered, so they order pancakes and sausage with apple juice. Rodney thinks to himself that he too is a little offended that she has not made an attempt to become intimate. Then unexpectedly, Renee asks Rodney if he has taken a shower yet or should she take one first. As Rodney is looking through his wallet to get the money to pay for the food delivery, he drops it in shock of her question. Renee lets out a huge laugh in response to him dropping his wallet. She knew then that Rodney was not ready for sex and asked if she startled him. Rodney says no, he just dropped his wallet, but Renee knew better than that. She was happy though, because she knew that they both were on the same page and neither of them was ready to have sex that night. Renee says that she'll take her shower first, better yet, she'll soak in the tub and that he can let her know when the food gets there. Rodney agrees and asks her if he can get comfortable, to which she replies yes. Rodney watches as she goes to the bathroom to soak, and let's off a sigh of relief. He can't believe that he was so scared to have sex but he knew that he wanted it to happen at the right place and at the right time, not because he feels pressure from his friends to do so. Maybe to their friends sex is just sex, but to Rodney he wants it to be special for him and Renee. He truly cares for her and feels that they will have a future together. If he has sex with her now, it will be done just to be cool or to impress his friends. The problem for Rodney in his mind is how he convinces Renee that he wants to wait until the time is right. Rodney checks his watch and realizes that it has been quite a long time since they ordered the food and since Renee went to soak in the tub. He knocks on the bathroom door to check on Renee. He does not get an answer. Worried, he knocks on the door again and asks Renee if she is ok. Renee replies that she is ok; she just dozed off for a little bit. The next minute Rodney hears a knock on the door. It's the deliveryman from the 24-hour restaurant next to the motel. He apologizes for the delay in bringing the food; he mentions that over 10 kids came in to the restaurant and with the limited staff for the late shift, that caused a delay in him delivering the food. Rodney laughs as he tells the deliveryman that he knows the kids and that they are all from his school. He pays the man and gives him a nice tip, then yells to Renee that the food is here. Renee acknowledges and thanks him for getting them both food. Renee exits from the bathroom with a lovely nightgown. All the kids were instructed to bring overnight clothes to the meet in the event that they were to stay overnight. The motel room had two beds; he put her order on her bed while he sat on Sarah's bed with his food. Rodney tells Renee that she looks incredible, especially since it is now 3 AM. Renee thanks him for the compliment and asks when Rodney will take his shower. Rodney laughs that he of course took one after the track meet but he said that he wants to take another one. Renee laughs, saying some guys feel they can treat girls anyway that they feel like. Rodney laughs with her and goes off to take his shower. Rodney exits to the bathroom, and at this time, Renee thinks to herself that she really wants to get intimate with Rodney, but she wants the first time to be perfect. She says she'll see what happens when he comes out the shower. A few minutes pass and Rodney exits the bathroom. While lying on Sarah's bed, Rodney mentions how good of a shower he had. Rodney asks how are her legs since they were aching earlier. Renee starts to tell him that they are fine but Rodney interrupts her. "Renee, everybody is expecting us to seize the moment and celebrate by having sex, which is something that I want to do but I don't want to have sex with you to satisfy Jeff, Sarah, or anybody else. I want us to do it for us". Rodney continues to tell her that he does not want to loose her as a girlfriend and that he wants their first time to be special, but if she wants to do it then he will to make her happy. By this time, Renee has sat up from the bed, as she is delighted to hear these words come from Rodney. Renee tells him that she is already happy to have a wonderful boyfriend who respects her and himself, and is willing to wait until the time is right. Renee admired Rodney's maturity and started to have feelings of love for him. Rodney thanks Renee and admits that he was nervous when he dropped his wallet. Renee burst out in laughter as she tells Rodney that she knew that already but it was cute. Rodney tells Renee that at an early age, his father taught him to always respect women and that he saw it first hand in the way his father treated Rodney's mother and stepmother. Rodney mentions that he does not want to get careless and slip up and have unprotected sex, I watch The Maury Povich show and I feel sorry for those kids. Rodney then jokes and says, "Rodney, you are the father". They both start laughing aloud. Renee chimes in and says who wants the burden of having children young and not being able to finish high school or college. Rodney agrees but interrupts by asking if he could at least have a nice kiss. Renee laughs and says that they both deserve it. Rodney approaches Renee's bed and reiterates how he wants their first time to be special and how his parents would kill him if he got a girl pregnant, they already have his college tuition waiting for him. They kiss and Renee says they should get some sleep before Sarah comes back. Rodney agrees and sets the alarm clock for 6 AM. They both then fall asleep on Renee's bed. At 5:30 AM, Sarah returns to the room. She knocks at first to let Rodney and Renee know that she is back. There is no answer. She opens the door and finds both of them asleep on Renee's bed. Sarah jokingly thinks to herself that she hopes Renee had a good experience because she had one with Jeff. The only concern is that Jeff did not want to use a condom so they had unprotected sex. After that night, Renee and Rodney's relationship began to take off. The rest of the school year went well for both of them and Rodney gave Renee a friendship ring. Unfortunately, Jeff found out that Sarah did get pregnant, as well as two other friends of Renee and Rodney. Jeff did not want to keep the child but Sarah decided she wanted to. Because of that, they both did not speak with each other anymore. One of the other couples decided to drop out of school to get jobs to support their child. Rodney and Renee stood by their friends and gave them support during this difficult time in their young lives. Rodney was devastated by hearing the news of Sarah and Jeff because he felt that they were two young people who had a bright future, but now their lives are changed forever because of one bad decision.

Young ladies and gentleman, these were two parallel stories of four young teenagers that have regular everyday situations, and making the wrong decisions in these situations can result in damaging results in your life. The only point of this story is that sex can wait; making irresponsible life altering decisions are not an option. The lives you hurt will be your own, and that of the child. A third story can be about the negative impact of being hooked on drugs. Some of our young mothers and fathers have to deal with addictions to marijuana, cocaine, or crack to name a few. Another scenario could include mothers dropping out of school and turning to prostitution to help support their children. Or the many headlines about mothers taking their babies lives to avoid having to deal with the responsibilities of being a parent. Let these stories help you think ahead, it really is not that hard to control your desires. Abstinence is not a bad thing either, please think about it!

As parents, we have to be prepared for all problems when we have children. One example is children with birth defects. Why would we as fathers not want to be there with the mothers to help deal with our children's issues? These are concerns that need both mom and dad's input and decision making. These children deserve the love and comfort of both parents. There also is the issue of homosexuality or bisexuality. How should parents react to this situation? Many people react very negatively to this subject matter. We all are God's children and deserve to be treated as such. Those of us who mistreat or abuse people for their race or sexual orientation, could be charged federally as discrimination on the bases of race or sexual orientation. It would be very unfair to abandon children with these issues in today's society. To avoid the mistreatment of people that may be different from us, be it our family member or our children and the like, there is counseling to help us properly deal with these issues and make the best decisions. The following are three stories that involve the possibility of such situations.

# The Ruth and Tom Peterson Story

Ruth and Tom Peterson are two excited parents anticipating their first child. Tom, a self-employed construction company owner, and Ruth, a partner at the Law firm Walsh, Peterson and Roberts, are upper middle class people who wanted to have children after they set themselves up financially and travel a bit. Tom worked long hours to get his company off the ground to make it profitable and has a moderately successful company. Ruth's firm is also quite successful, given the fact that lawyers are always in need for one reason or another. They build their home in the residential area just outside of Stanford Connecticut, and both commute to New York City. Ruth prepared herself to work from home for the first year after having the baby to enjoy the joys of being a full-time mother. Tom worked around asbestos and other unhealthy substances that come with the construction business. Tom's doctor had been warning him for years to be careful of various contaminants in the construction business, but Tom, being a hands on guy, persisted in his hands on style. Ruth on the other hand was very careful with her health prior to getting pregnant because she wanted her first baby to be born with the least amount of complications. In fact, Ruth was a health food, vitamin, and exercise fanatic. Ruth had a gym built in their home next to the den. Tom rarely used the gym; instead, he developed a smoking habit on top of his construction exposures at work. The pressure of his job, in combination with the smoking, affected his blood pressure as well. As Ruth approached her third month of pregnancy, she noticed spotting when she used the toilet. She ignored it the first time because it was light. The next day she noticed it again. After a brief workout and shower, this time it was a little heavier and she eased up on her workout. Ruth brought her concerns to Tom's attention but he just brushed it off and said not to be alarmed.

With that, Ruth decided not to tell her doctor, Doctor Benjamin. Ruth did ease up on her workouts and took shorter walks, and the spotting did stop. She was four and a half-months and began feeling erratic and movements from the baby. This happened while Ruth was with a client in her office. She began to lose her color and feeling faint. Her client ran out the office and summoned her secretary who ran into her boss's office; her boss took one look at her and called Tom to meet Ruth at the hospital. Tom called her doctor and began his trek to the hospital. After putting his site manager in charge, Tom takes out a cigarette and popped a pressure pill at the same time. Tom got angry with Ruth, thinking she might have overdid it with her workouts that's causing the problems that she is having now. Ruth arrives at the hospital but her spotting returns, this time it's a constant bleeding that is beginning to worry the emergency room doctors. Doctor Benjamin is in surgery and couldn't make it to the hospital to meet Ruth and Tom. Tom left his job site but didn't know which hospital the EMS took his wife, so he called Ruth's secretary to find out. Twenty minutes later, Tom arrives at the hospital, forty-five minutes after Ruth's arrival. He visits Ruth in an emergency room where he learns that Ruth lost a little blood and the baby is being monitored but his condition has stabilized. Tom awaits the doctor's update on his wife's condition; meanwhile Tom calls his parents and Ruth's parents to inform them of the day's events. While speaking to Ruth's mother, the emergency room doctor, Doctor Thompson, comes with updates. Tom interrupts his conversation with his mother-in-law to listen to the doctor but tells her that he'll put the doctor on speaker so we can hear her condition together. Ruth's mom eagerly accepts the idea with open arms. Dr. Thompson, also a woman, says, "Hello, are you Mr. Tom Peterson"? Tom responds, "Yes ma'am, I am". Dr. Thompson continues, "Your wife and baby are doing fine now, the baby is having a few unexpected problems, it's a boy by the way". The doctor continues, "He is having problems that we can't figure out yet, I just want to ask you a few questions about your health". She adds, "Your wife's health is terrific". Tom replies "Yes doctor, ask away". The doctor replies, "Thanks, tell me when was the last time you had a check up"? Tom responds "A month ago". The doctor continues, "I mean a complete check-up". Tom again responds a month ago. Dr. Thompson asks him what was the outcome. Tom began slowly by saying "Well, I have high blood pressure and due to my work..." The doctor interrupted and asks, "What is that Mr. Peterson"? He responds, "Construction work, I sometimes come in contact with asbestos and other contaminants. My doctor wants me to; oh, by the way I smoke. And he wants me to stop". Dr. Thompson tells him that many health characteristics carry over to your children and we're hoping that your child is not suffering because of some bad health characteristics that may come from his parents. She goes on to say "Mr. Peterson, she is resting right now so you can visit her within the hour, but may I call your doctor to get your medical records"? Tom agrees to give her his doctor's information before he leaves. Tom slowly gets back on the cell phone with his mother-in-law. He takes her off speaker and says, "Well, you heard her mom". His mother-in-law responds "Yes Tom, let's hope Ruth gets better quickly and tell her that I love her, ok son". Tom responds, "Yes mom". Tom, while in the waiting room, sits back in his chair, puts his hands on his heart and says in a quiet tone not to disturb the others in the waiting room "Wow, I hope my years of not being health conscious and properly taking care of myself like I should does not affect my child's health". Tom immediately looks up his personal physician's phone number and begins the process of getting his medical information to Dr. Thompson. He also decides not return to work, but to stay with his wife at the hospital. An hour later, Dr. Thompson has reviewed Ruth's test results and decides to check her in for further test and monitor her reaction to certain medications. After about two hours from her arrival, Ruth begins to awake from being medicated. She realized that she was in a hospital bed in her own room. She looked over to her left and noticed her husband asleep, and called his name. Tom hears his name being called and jumps up thinking he was dreaming. "Ruth" he yells, "Oh my God, how are you"? Ruth breaks out in a yell "Tommy, did I lose my baby? Did I?" Tom responds, "No honey, he's fine". Ruth ask what happened and Tom responds, choosing his words carefully " Your doctor, Dr. Thompson, decided to keep you overnight and monitor the medication and your reaction to it. Also, they want a background of my medical history". Ruth asks why they would be interested in his health records, "I'm having the baby, not you, and my health is fine". Tom says, "Ruth, you are absolutely right, but honey it takes two to make babies. You supply the eggs, I supply the sperm, and my health is just as important". Ruth listened and responded "Yes Dear, sometimes we women forget that. So did you cooperate with their request or did they ask for your medical information"? Tom, while staring out of the hospital room window, responds "Yes and yes. Yes they asked for my records and yes I cooperated". Tom turns to Ruth, walks to her bed, and leans over and gives her a kiss on the forehead. "Honey, everything is going to be alright, I promise. Everything is going to be alright"! As Tommy is still leaning over Ruth, Dr. Thompson walks in. "Hello folks", she says. Ruth and Tom respond, "How are you doctor"? Dr. Thompson responds "Fine thanks. Mrs. Peterson, I decided to keep you overnight to monitor your reaction to two different medications I've given you. Also, your husband was willing to allow us to look at his medical background to see if there is anything we should know. Your health is fine, but your baby is showing signs of a rare malfunction or disorder, and before we conclude, we want to look at his past and present health records. Don't worry, so far the baby is okay, as you see you are well connected with enough monitors and we're keeping an eye on everything. Any questions"? Ruth asks if there is any chance of them losing the baby? Dr. Thompson pauses and chooses her words very carefully, and then replies "Don't think about that Mrs. Peterson, that will only worry you more. I wouldn't worry about that". Ruth feels she can't help but to worry. Dr. Thompson assures her that both she and the baby will be fine and that her doctor will be there shortly. Dr. Thompson says, "It was a pleasure meeting you both and Dr. Keith will begin to see you. He is my replacement. Take care". Tom and Ruth both say thank you very much. Both Ruth and Tom embrace again and say a little prayer. She stays the night with Tom by her side. She was instructed to go home and stay in bed for the next two days, and depending on the spotting and how she felt, she would be able to resume her normal schedule. Tom, very worried about the baby's health, began to change a few of his own health habits by working out more in the gym and watching what he eats. He also stopped smoking knowing that might be hard, but a good idea to do so. As Tom and Ruth Peterson's life began to get back to normal and Ruth spending two to three days working from home, they are well into her sixth month of pregnancy. It's been decided by Ruth's doctor that Tom needs to get a check-up to review his blood disorder. Tom and Ruth's doctor noticed an overlooked problem with a blood test result that was not looked at more carefully. Tom's doctor apologized for his oversight of the test, and will inform him and his wife of his findings. Meanwhile, Ruth felt a little unusual movement, kicking and bumping around in spurts. She is now in her seventh month and Tom just received a phone call to come to his doctor's office alone. Not to worry his wife, he agreed to drop by the next day. Ruth saw Tom's expression after hanging up his cell phone. She asked "Tom, who was that"? Tom replied, " Oh, it was my doctor". Ruth asks why he didn't call the house number. Tom responds, "I don't know honey, I didn't ask him". Ruth asked what did he want, which Tom replies, "He asked how were you feeling". Ruth realized that if he wanted to know that, he could have called the house phone. She knew something was up. Ruth knew that Tom would protect her and not want her to worry, so she took the house phone in the den and called Tom's doctor. She asked to speak to Tom's doctor, Dr. Walter Johnson. They exchanged greetings and Ruth says, "Tom and I have been married for thirteen years. I know when he is worried about something, and Walter he is concerned about me and his health". Dr. Johnson replies, "Ruth, no one can fool you lawyers. I only asked him to come and see me tomorrow. You can come with him Ruth, ok". Ruth responds, "It doesn't sound good Walter, should I worry". Dr. Johnson responds "No Ruth, just hug him and tell him that he is the most fortunate man in the world to have a wife like you, and that we spoke today". Ruth went over to Tom, who was sitting on the porch, and said, "Tom, we are in this together, I spoke to your doctor and he wants us both to see him tomorrow. Thank you for trying to not make me worry, we'll get through this together". While Ruth and Tom embrace, he was there for her in the hospital, and now she is there for him. It's obvious that they truly love each other, and whatever happens in their lives, they will be there for each other. The next day, both Tom and Ruth arrive at the doctor's office holding hands. The spotting and erratic movement in Ruth had subsided. Dr. Johnson thanked them for coming and said, "You two are picture perfect, and support each other very well. So I'm glad that you both are here. First, Ruth how are you feeling"? Ruth tells the doctor that she has her good and bad days, and then asks how is Tommy. The doctor replies, "He will be put on special medication to stabilize his red blood cells". Ruth says, that she is not worried about Tom, she is worried about the baby, Dr. Johnson continues that both parents can pass their health issues to their off spring. At this point, Tom will think health. He tells Ruth that she has a team of good doctors and that she is very healthy, adding that he wishes both he and Tom were as healthy as she was. But he wanted to return the focus on the baby. The Petersons stood-up, thanked the doctor, and walked out the same way they walked in, holding hands. They know that this pregnancy will test their love, and marriage, because they both really want to have this baby. They arrive home when Ruth realized that the movement of the baby has been a bit abnormal since she left the hospital. Every now and then the baby moves erratically. Ruth's obstetrician has been having Ruth visit her once a week since her hospital visit. The doctor believes the baby is showing signs that it will have a little abnormality. His vital signs are not normal, and she wants to sit down with both Ruth and Tom to break the news. Doctor Monica Alvarez believed she saw the abnormalities for at least two weeks, but didn't want to break the news to them because of the other health issues Tom was having. Dr. Alvarez told Ruth that next week when she comes, to bring Tom with her so she can discuss the baby's progress with both of them. Ruth agreed and had Tom make himself available the night before they were to meet Dr. Alvarez. They had dinner at home, but both were quiet and very nervous. Ruth, having not felt any movement in a couple of hours, thought to herself that he must have been having a long sleep. Another hour passes, nothing. She thought to herself "What time is it"? It was six pm and she thought that she would lay down for a couple of hours and he'll be sure to be awake, no reason to panic. She tells Tom that she is going to lie down and ask if he is alright. Tom responds that he is fine and asks how is she. She responds, "The baby has been quiet for a couple of hours, I'm going to get some rest, ok". Tom responds "ok". Tom goes to the gym for some exercise; he spends an hour on the treadmill. While working out, he says, "Wow, I have a lot of work to do, my breath is short, and my body is killing me". At about 9:30 in the evening, Tom hears a loud scream from their bedroom. Tom immediately stops his workout, and runs to the bedroom. He asks Ruth what is the matter. Ruth responds, "I woke up to use the bathroom and noticed blood in the bed, and my abdomen feels very heavy, like dead weight. Call the ambulance"! Tom calls 911, "Operator, operator, please send an ambulance. I think my wife is losing the baby. Please hurry"! The operator tells Mr. Peterson that the ambulance is on the way. Within five minutes, an ambulance arrives, and Tom lets them upstairs. They immediately give Ruth oxygen and work on her. They notice no activity from the baby. They immediately rush Ruth to the emergency room. Tom follows down behind the ambulance with tears streaming down his face, feeling that the problems that they are having with the pregnancy is because of his bad health. Within thirteen minutes, they arrive at the emergency room. The medical team was expecting her arrival and start working to save the baby. Tom paces the waiting room nervous and anxious, wanting to go out and have a smoke but given his health issues, says that is the last thing he needs now. After forty minutes, Tom becomes very impatient and stands by the emergency room door. Another twenty minutes pass, and Tom says to himself "Please God, help me stay strong for her and the baby, help me be there for her no matter what happens". Another twelve minutes passes and the door opens slowly, and the team walks out. As the doctors come out of the operating room, Tom slowly sits in the nearest seat and stares off into space expecting the worse. They quietly say hello Mr. Peterson. The lead doctor says Ruth is fine. When he heard that, he literally broke out in tears, knowing that if the baby were fine, he would have said both Ruth and the baby are fine. Tom knew. He slowly got up and walked down the hall, with one doctor who had his hand on his back. Even the doctor's eyes were wet. They know that they would have to get Mr. and Mrs. Peterson counseling as soon as possible. Dr. Alvarez was called and made aware of the situation. The recovery from the lost and the counseling was very hard. Tom wanted their child very badly. They waited so long, they prepared so well. Dr. Alvarez had Ruth and Tom to receive the best counseling money could buy, they needed it. Tom was very critical of his health problems. This process took both Ruth and Tom weeks to get back on their feet, mentally and emotionally. After six weeks of being in a support group and getting constant counseling, they slowly recovered because Ruth was there for Tom and Tom was there for Ruth. As they planned their future, Tom started being mindful of his health. After two year, they had their new baby, and began helping other couples handle the lost of a child by joining support groups.

Young teenage women and men, think outside the box. Young men, when you see a young lady of interest, first look at her as a lovely human being, as hard as it may be. I'll give you that, I was a young teen and young adult. But look at her as a lovely woman that you should and must respect, and not as a piece of meat. Think first, generation after generation people don't seem to understand, if you have unprotected sex, she might get pregnant. Am I ready to be a father? Young ladies, don't forget that you have the power. Don't abuse that power; keep in mind it's your game to lose. Think outside the box, if we have unprotected sex, A) I might get a disease, B) I might get pregnant, C) Am I ready to be a mom, and D) It's about the baby, once it comes, it's here. Think about it!

This next story tackles the issue of homosexuality. As parents, we must be prepared to face this issue and react lovingly and sensibly.

# The Story of Ron and Tony Jr.

Loraine and Tony Bryant Sr. lived modestly in a town where they stick together and look out for each other. They have two daughters and one son. Their oldest child is Teresa, second is Tony Jr., and their third is Lisa. They are the ages of eighteen, seventeen, and fourteen respectively. Teresa is an outgoing and sociable teenager with lots of friends. Her mother wants her to go to college and get her degree before getting serious with a boyfriend. She believes that getting serious at this age would only distract her from her goals. Both parents want their children to be educated and prepared to support themselves. Teresa dates occasionally, but as soon as it starts to get serious, she either breaks it off or begins to act erratically to make her boyfriend back off or think that she can't go beyond a certain point in a relationship. Theresa had a very special relationship last year, when she was seventeen, that began to get very serious and he didn't want to just be friends. He wanted more, and Teresa knew that it would have created a big problem with her parents. His name is Tyrone. Teresa still stays in touch with him because he's still the one young man that she truly likes. Teresa wants to be a plastic surgeon. She's a pre-med student and has excellent grades; she's made the honor roll in every grade in high school and is a shooting star. Tony Bryant Jr. is a quiet and soft-spoken young man who is closer to his mother than his father. His father is very athletic and enjoys football on Sunday. He also was an amateur boxer in his youth. Tony Jr. wants to be an engineer. Being a junior in high school, his guidance counselor is guiding him through all of his courses. Since he is the only male child, his mother spoils him and he gets what he wants from her. The father on the other hand, spoils the girls. Keeping to their agenda of keeping the kids focused on higher education and college. After high school, the father never discusses with Tony the "G" subject, or Girls, Girls, Girls, but he expects him to at least talk about them, have a lady friend to call, or go out occasionally. Tony Sr. is a "Be There Father". His goal is to create success in youth, and in his spare time, he is a community organizer, helping young men in his community keep their eyes on being better and responsible men. When Tony Sr. does these things, he asks his son to go with him and encourage young men his age and younger since he is a good role model. Tony Jr.'s interest in engineering would no doubt encourage other young men to pursue or have a similar goal. This particular night, Tony Jr. accompanies his father to one such event. While going, both father and son decide to walk. It's a clear but hot night, and as they walk and talk, a lovely young lady passes them by. She's dressed for the weather, shorts and a blouse. Tony Sr. thought to himself "Wow, what a lovely young lady", and continued to walk and talk to his son. The father noticed that his son had literally no reaction, not even a simple acknowledgement. Mr. Bryant thought nothing of it; they proceeded to the evenings activities, which turned out to be a very productive night. They had group sessions with young men, encouraged them to do well in school, and not to stay out on the streets late because that could lead to trouble. Lisa, the baby girl, is a big fan of Tyra Banks; she wants to be a model. Her mother thinks that Ms. Banks is a good role model for young girls and teenage women, she survived the divorce of her parents and went on to become a super model. She also went on from there to become a TV talk show host, and created her own TV modeling show "Americas Next Top Model". Lisa also liked the singer and actress Miley Cyrus, who became a success at an early age following in her father's footsteps. Lisa thought that she didn't need to go to college; all she had to do was learn how to sing, dance and act. She believed that she could learn to on her own. Both Mr. and Mrs. Bryant believed that they had a little more time to convince her to still pursue college and make entertainment an extra-curricular activity. Lisa had to be pushed to live up to her potential. Lorraine Bryant, had Lisa's guidance counselor to get her assistance to focus and take her studies more seriously. Teresa graduates and decided to begin her college career locally to get a feel for college life before she thinks about going away to school and get the best possible education for her time and money. Tony Jr. was approaching his graduation and his father feels now is the time to sit down with him and discuss the "Birds and the Bees" on a serious level. Mr. Bryant asked Tony Jr. to meet him in the den in thirty minutes. Tony Jr. agrees. Thirty minutes later, in comes Tony Jr. who says, "What's up Pop"? Mr. Bryant tells his son to sit down and says, "First of all, I want to thank you and your sisters for your fine scholastic achievements as well as no drugs, jail, or baby momma and daddy drama. For that, both your mother and I are very pleased. Your uncles and I started the girl thing a little earlier, and I applaud your patience on this subject. You are about to enter your senior year, do you have any questions about young ladies and their concerns? What's your opinion of women in general? What kind of women do you like"? Tony Jr. leans back in his chair, takes a deep breath, and stares into space. Tony Jr. reflects back to his elementary days, while sitting in class when the prettiest girl in his class liked him and sent a note to him. The note simply read "Tony I like you". That's when it dawned on him that his feelings for women were different from most boys. Once the other boys found out that the girl, who's name was Gail Ryan, liked him and that it didn't make his day, they knew something was different about Tony Jr. That's when he wanted answers himself as to "why he didn't feel the same say about Gail Ryan as the other boys did"? There was another situation when the girls elected him the most popular boy in his entire grade, but that didn't faze him. It was no big deal. On the other hand, he enjoyed playing basketball, baseball, and soccer with the guys. On another occasion, he had to make a choice between going to a girl's house after school or visiting a male friend who was home sick from school and he chose his sick male friend, he felt that it was no contest. Tony Jr. also knew the real reason why he wanted to play basketball last year because he was attracted to the team captain. At the age of seventeen approaching eighteen, he was clearly more attracted to men than women. Then the question is "how can I tell my father the desire to sleep with a woman is just not there"? When Audrey Taylor grabbed my hand, I automatically, without thinking twice, pulled my hand back. That was very awkward. In fact, the basketball team captain, Ronald Bradley, agreed to go to the same college and that we get an apartment together. Back to the discussion with his father, Tony Jr. responds to his father's question "Pop, you and mom taught me to be very selective about women and not to rush into any relationships. Women are beautiful and I think that one day I'll settle down and get into a relationship. Maybe not this upcoming semester, I don't want to be distracted". Tony Sr. smiled and said to his son "Good son, I respect that answer. First things first, girls are not going anywhere". Mr. Bryant gets up and says quietly "Wow, I was a little nervous for a minute, that's my boy". Meanwhile, Tony Jr. said to himself "This buys me a little time to figure this out. Talk to mom, my guidance counselor, maybe see a doctor. I never acted on my feelings, but I wanted to and not with a woman. Mom, as a woman, seems like she knows but is waiting for me to confide in her about my feelings. But before I speak to mom, I want to speak to Mrs. Feldman (the eleventh grade guidance counselor). Over the next couple of weeks, Tony Jr. became very withdrawn and quiet at dinner and other family functions. He became less and less available for his father's community activities. He decided to make an appointment to see Mrs. Feldman to discuss his feelings and figure out what to do. The meeting with Mrs. Feldman was on a Tuesday morning at 10 AM. Over the loud speaker, Tony was called to report to the Guidance Counselors office. Tony was excused from class for the rest of the class, and eventually was excused from all of his classes for the day. Tony walked in Mrs. Feldman's office. "Good morning Mrs. Feldman" Tony said. "Hello Tony" she responded, "How can I help you"? Before he could answer, Mrs. Feldman interrupts "I reviewed your records and you are doing well. It looks like you will graduate with honors like your big sister Teresa; I wish most of my students were as easy to get along with, like you and your sister. The other kids in the school are good too, just that you and your sister are outstanding. With that said Tony, how can I help you"? Tony replies, "Thank you for your time Mrs. Feldman, how do I start"? In less than a year, I'm going to be eighteen, I've never had a girlfriend, and I never wanted one. I believe that I'm not attracted to women sexually. When growing up in grade school, when the guys were talking about their girlfriends or how they wanted to have girlfriends, I made up stories about girls to not feel left out. When girls showed an interest in me, I always found a way to elude them or make excuses not to be with them. When I was younger, all of my crushes were on young male stars on TV. I never wanted to play with dolls but I use to like women's clothes better than the usual male clothing. Pretty crazy huh"? Mrs. Feldman was taking notes and when he asked her that question, she only said, "Tony, that's not crazy, that's the way you felt, then it's not crazy". That response from Mrs. Feldman really made Tony relax. Mrs. Feldman asked him "Do you want some water, soda or something"? Tony responded, "Yes Mrs. Feldman, my throat is a little dry". She says, "Take five minutes and come back". Tony then went to the cafeteria and got a soda, went to the bathroom and returned to the guidance counselor's office. When Tony returns to Mrs. Feldman's office, she was on the phone talking to another school official about another student. She told Tony to come in and take a seat. After five minutes on the phone, Mrs. Feldman apologized to Tony and resumed their conversation. She asked, "How do you feel"? Tony responded "Surprisingly, very comfortable Mrs. Feldman". He continued, "The last thing I want to do is disappoint my parents". Mrs. Feldman quickly responds, "Right now Tony, this is about a young man being true to himself. There is a place in this world for everybody. Please continue". Tony thanks Mrs. Feldman for her comment and says, "That's it, there are more things I can tell you, but I think you see my situation". Mrs. Feldman replies, "Well Tony, I do. Is it alright if I can ask you some questions"? Tony says yes. She continues, "Do you think you're gay"? Tony responds that seems to be the case. She continues, "Would you want to speak to another school official? I take it you haven't spoken to your parents yet". Tony quietly responds, "No I haven't said a word to either of my parents but I think my mother might have an idea". Mrs. Feldman continues, "Well Tony, the last thing you need to think is that there is something wrong with you. Again, would you want to discuss this with any other staff members before I make a recommendation"? Tony responds not really, only if she thinks he should. She replies, "Well Tony, this is what I would like to do, and that is approach your parents about it and if you really don't know if you are gay or not, I recommend someone to help you figure it out". Tony responds "Ok. At this point, I truly believe that you have my best interest at heart, so I'm willing to work with you and follow your recommendations". At that, Mrs. Feldman assures him that he did the right thing by approaching her. Many parents, due to a lack of understanding or not knowing how to respond to this matter, might react with hostility. Many young people might not feel that they are normal and leave home, and find comfort in the wrong person or just give up school, life, or everything. Just go home, continue with your normal routine and I'll let you know when I'll make an appointment to speak to them. She asks would he want to be present when they come. Tony responds "Not really Mrs. Feldman". Within a week, Mrs. Feldman made an appointment with his parents after getting in touch with professionals on this matter; she met with Mr. and Mrs. Bryant. The next week on Thursday evening, Mrs. Feldman thanks the Bryant's for their time and interest in their son's progress. She starts off "How are you both doing"? They respond "very good". She continues "Your son Tony is doing excellently as you know, and he is looking forward to graduating and studying for a degree in engineering. Do you folks have any questions"? Mr. Bryant says "Yes, just a quick one. I know we have plenty of time but please give us a listing of the best local engineering colleges in our area just to get him started". She replies, "You got it". She then continues, "I've known you folks for a few years; I know all your children and you have three of the best I've seen. Tony approached me last week and wanted to meet with me to discuss a situation that he's going through. He expressed deep love for both of you and never wants to disappoint you, but he is having a personal conflict about his sexuality'. Mrs. Bryant made a small sigh. With her head leaning back, she reaches over and grabs the hand of her husband. Mr. Bryant jumps up and grabs his head, then stares out the window. Mrs. Feldman goes over, sits next to Mrs. Bryant, and holds her hand. Mrs. Feldman then goes over to the phone, calls her secretary, and asks her to bring in Mrs. Baldwin. Mrs. Baldwin specializes in family therapy and wanted to be present if she was needed. Mrs. Baldwin comes in and reaches out to Mr. Bryant, who is still starring out the window. Mrs. Feldman and Baldwin give them a minute to collect themselves and settle down. After ten minutes, Mr. Bryant asked to be alone with his wife. Both Mrs. Feldman and Baldwin quickly agreed. They were told to take their time, and Mr. and Mrs. Bryant hugged and told each other how much they loved each other. After about fifteen minutes, Mr. Bryant went out to get the ladies to begin addressing their son's concerns. He says, "We love our son, and that's what counts". Mrs. Feldman says "Thank you for coming Mr. and Mrs. Bryant. After speaking to your son Tony last week, I consulted with our school district's psychologist. Mrs. Baldwin will answer any questions you may have and make a few recommendations. Mrs. Baldwin, thank you". Mrs. Baldwin begins speaking "Hello Mr. and Mrs. Bryant, my name is Claire Baldwin, district 29 child and youth psychologist. I went over the notes Mrs. Feldman took when speaking to your son last week. First of all, he loves and respects you both very much. Mr. Bryant, you are his hero. Mrs. Bryant, you are mom so there is no replacing you. With that said, your child is a regular, everyday, intelligent young man and should be treated as such. That's my job, to protect children and work with parents to accomplish that goal. I will answer any concerns you may have and help you understand what your son is going through. Your son reached out, a lot of people leave home, quit school, turn to drugs, etc. This is done just to not have to face their families, and their fear of not being understood. Tony said that he wasn't sure if he was gay, so the first thing I suggest that we all get together at some point and begin counseling. But first, let me recommend an associate to prepare you to accept the possibility of him being gay while we find out directly from him while working with him further. Do you folks have any questions thus far"? Mr. Bryant responded "Yes Mrs. Baldwin, as well as for you Mrs. Feldman. This is a shock to us I must admit, but we love our son, and my wife and I will work with your office and we look forward to your recommendations in the future". Mrs. Baldwin responds, "I'm sure Tony would be pleased to know that his parents still love him and are willing to understand what he's going through. And with your permission, Mrs. Feldman and I would like to continue to win his confidence and really find out if he is really gay or not. And if he is, we want to help him move on with his life and make him not feel that he is anything less than human than any other human being. And last but not least, please treat him the same and don't make him feel uncomfortable. Also, hold off from telling the girls until we find out just what's going on with his true sexuality. Mrs. Bryant, do you have any questions at this point"? Mrs. Bryant responds "No. As a mother, you have intuition or a feeling, but just couldn't put your finger on something and you're just not sure. Thank you ladies for everything. Please keep us up to date". After leaving the guidance counselors office, Mr. and Mrs. Bryant went to get lunch to further discuss their strategy in regards to this revelation of their son possibly being homosexual. Both doctors inform Tony Jr. of their meeting with his parents and that they are working with them and appreciate his honesty, and that they love him very much. With that vote of confidence, Tony's spirits were lifted and he thanked the ladies and went back to class. After two weeks of consulting with Tony and having him to truly confront his feelings, Tony came to the conclusion that he was sure that he was gay and that he would inform his parents. Meanwhile Mr. and Mrs. Bryant followed the doctor's recommendations over the last two weeks and were ready to accept Tony's lifestyle. The girls were also offered counseling if they felt they needed it. At Tony's request, he met with the whole family and broke the news to his sisters. They hugged him and told him that they loved him and would treated him the same as before. They attended a few sessions of counseling to further understand the lifestyle. Tony Jr. encouraged Ronald, his friend who was the basketball team captain, to also come out. Ron did; he met with the guidance counselor and Dr. Baldwin. Ron's father didn't want to accept or understand his son's feelings and eventually ordered Ron to leave his house. After graduation, Ron's mother supported her son and said to her husband "If Ron goes, so do I". With that, Ron's father thought about it and tried harder to understand his son and accepted counseling. Ron and Tony went on to college, lived their lives, and became everyday citizens in their community. Being a parent of three children, once my wife got pregnant, I began to prepare myself for any and everything, and as you read in this book, we had three very unpredictable pregnancies and deliveries. It always helps, as parents, to be there for each other. At this time, I would like to remind the readers of this book that I tell these stories to let the reader visualize each point that I want to make. If a young lady can see herself in a similar situation, that is how she may want to go as oppose to heading down the wrong track or if she decides to head down the track, just what might be the result. Also with young men, there are points in these stories for them to think about. We don't want our young adults to make a bad decision that will ruin their lives, as well as the young ladies or their children. Everyone has a choice in life, and once you become an adult, be it eighteen or twenty-one, you are responsible for your actions. Also, when you make a major mistake of having a child too early in life, you bring stress to your parents who have to raise both you and your child. That's not fair to you, your parents, to the young lady, and especially the child. The court system will look out for the innocent child. Please think before you act. Please young ladies, the power is yours to protect your own bodies, to dictate your future. Don't forget, if you don't have self-respect, most young men won't respect you either. You both must remember, unprotected sex is for two adults who know what they are doing. The mother of my children had three children by the age of twenty-eight and her first child at nineteen, but she was married to a caring husband and father to her kids. A man who had a job and was brought up very religious, in fact, we met at a religious function. Ladies, don't be afraid to be an "I just want to be a wait a while young lady". And young men, always attempt to be a "Be there for my kids and their mother father". Let's make a commitment to ourselves, to break the cycle of self-destruction in our society by not ruining our lives, the lives of young women, and our unloved and not properly cared for children. The last story in this book will underline the point of having a child that may have a birth defect. We salute those parents who keep their children, although knowing that they may have an impending defect. When you have children, anything can happen. Both mother and father should be present in that child's life don't you think?

# The Story of Miguel and Anna Rodriguez

The baby shower was planned perfectly. Anna's sister was able to keep Anna out of the house all day while Miguel, Anna's parents, and their first child Rebecca decorated the basement with balloons. Anna, a Hospital Administrator, and Miguel, an Architect, live in a beautiful upscale neighborhood outside of Houston Texas. They don't live far from Anna's hospital, Houston Memorial. Miguel, while putting up ribbons form the ceiling, received a phone call from one of his contractors confirming an appointment for the following Monday to meet and discuss their next project for the following month, May. Mr. Rodriguez is responsible for six of Houston's largest skyscrapers and has the awards all over his home office to prove his handy work. It's 4:30 in the afternoon, when the doorbell rings and the company Party Time USA arrives with food, which Anna's mother directs them to the backyard. Their backyard is just under one and a half acres. The company also supplies chairs, outside decorations and music. By 6:00, the house is ready. All of the guests were asked to be present before 6:30. As the last guest arrives, the phone rings and its Anna's sister, Yvette. Yvette asks if she and her sister can begin to head to the house. Their mother says yes, the timing is perfect and the house is ready. Anna comes out of the rest room and says, "Yvette, I'm tired and this baby is kicking like crazy. Are you ready to take me home"? Yvette replies, "Yes I am, Mario is hungry and he wants me to bring home some Kentucky Fried Chicken". Everything is ready and all of the visitors park around the corner of the house, out of Anna's sight. Yvette was told what streets to avoid. Anna's father couldn't attend due to being ill. It's now 6:45 in the evening and Yvette was asked to pull in the driveway. As everyone listens for the car, the lookout yelled, "They're here"! Miguel yells, "Alright everyone, quiet please". Yvette pulls into the driveway, but they both are involved in a very important discussion about their father's health. As the ladies take the bags out of the car, Yvette ask Anna "Before I run home, may I take a look at the Lilies in your yard? I like how you have them arranged". Anna replies "Absolutely". They begin the walk to the backyard and Anna asks, "What's that I smell, someone is barbequing, and it smells good". "Surprise", everyone yells out loud. Anna drops her bags in total amazement. They start the music and Miguel sneaks up behind her, turns her around and says, "Ha ha, we got you". Anna breaks out in tears of joy. "Oh my god Miguel, this was a total surprise and everything is so beautiful! Who designed the yard"? Miguel says "Your neighbors Robin, MaryAnn, and Rebecca". They partied, celebrated, and opened gifts until 11:30 that night. Anna was getting tired and the kids were literally falling asleep in the yard. Anna thanked everyone for all they did, "We really appreciate your time and effort, and Yes, the food was delicious". Everyone had a good time and wished them well with the baby. Anna approaches her seventh month and she is at her obstetrician's office. He gives her a clean bill of health. The baby is in the right position; heartbeat is normal, etc. The Rodriguez's are expecting a son and the guest at the baby shower bring gifts with that in mind. Anna, now in her eight month, decided to take a one-year leave to recover and enjoy the baby. She had a big baby shower from her coworkers and former patients from her days as a head nurse. The Rodriguez's are a happy couple, and they are greatly anticipating their son. Miguel and Anna want to name him after Miguel's father, Hector, who was killed in Vietnam when Miguel was a little boy. His mother never got over her husband's death. Miguel became an architect like his father, after Miguel grew up, he changed his middle name to Hector in honor of his late father. Mr. Hector Rodriquez received a Purple Heart for his bravery in leading his command of eleven men into harms way to save the lives of thirty-three fellow soldiers. Hector was killed along with two other soldiers. Miguel is a very proud son. Both Anna and Miguel will name their son Hector Miguel Rodriguez. This made his mother very proud and happy. The baby is due in three weeks and everyone is anxious and wants to be there for Anna. This will also be the first male grandson of his mother and late father. The due date of September 18th arrives and there is no Hector yet. On September 18th at about 10:00 in the morning, the phone rings. It's Anna's mother and she asks if Anna is in labor yet. Anna replies "No momma, no labor". Anna's mother ask where is Miguel and Anna tells her he is at work on stand-by. Her mother replies, "That's good. Is he moving around"? Ana replies yes, and her mother says good and tells her that she and Yvette will see her later. Nothing happens for the rest of the day and Anna becomes restless. The entire night and next day nothing occurs. The doctor tells her to do plenty of walking, which she does. Going into the night of the 20th, early in the morning she begins labor. She remembers the feeling! It's 5:00 AM and Anna wakes Miguel. Miguel calls Yvette and begins the process of getting ready to go to the hospital. The arrangements are for Miguel to call Yvette, alert the rest of the family, and then call the doctor to meet them at the hospital. They arrive at the hospital emergency room and the doctors take her in. After an examination, they confirm that she is in labor. The ER doctor wanted Anna to walk a little and to time her contractions. They do what the doctor instructs, Miguel kept track of her contractions, and in the process, they ran into her family while pacing the halls of the hospital. "Hey Folks" Miguel says to Anna's family. "Meet us in the Labor and Delivery; the doctor wants us to walk a little. She's not ready yet". After about twenty-minutes of walking, they sat down. The contractions were steady and were becoming closer. Miguel then checked with the doctor and he said to have her come back in and let's check her out. Miguel then brought Anna in and they put her on the monitor, he noticed that the baby was having distress. The heartbeat was faint and as he looked closer, the baby had the umbilical cord around his neck. The doctor ordered an immediate C-section. After a sixty-five minute operation, the baby survived but may have encountered some damage because the cord caused the baby to be under an extended length of distress, which concerned the doctor. By the time Anna's doctor arrived, the baby had already been delivered. Her doctor consulted with the doctor who delivered the baby. There was concern that the baby might have long-term complications. Both Anna and the baby stayed an extra couple of days in the hospital for evaluation. Anna was released after three days but they kept little Miguel to run further test, he had a form of spina bifida. When Anna was released, the family had planned a coming home party for Anna and the baby, but they cancelled because no one was in a festive mood. Instead, they sat around and supported each other realizing the possibility of the baby having permanent damage. Unfortunately, after a number of additional test, it was determined that little Hector Miguel had spina bifida, but not the most severe form. Hector Miguel Rodriguez suffered a disorder that will be with him for the rest of his life. It will take this very close, tight knit family, all the love and patience to get through this life-altering ordeal. Two professional upper-middle class people who worked hard, played by the rules in life, did right by others, never blamed anyone for their misfortune. They realize that it's going to take the cooperation of Anna, Miguel, their daughter, and the rest of the family to give them all of the moral support that they may need. In cases like these, many people would not hesitate to give the baby up for adoption, but these two grown and responsible adults decided to keep their child with special needs and raised their child themselves. Young adults, this is something to think about.

## Giving Back/Heroes

While growing up, it is always good to have heroes to look up to. In my day, we had Rosa Parks, Thurgood Marshall, Martin Luther King and Coretta Scott King, Jesse Jackson, Andrew Young, Maynard Jackson,

Julian Bond, Sammy Davis Jr., Berry Gordy, Aretha Franklin, Gladys Knight, President Lyndon B. Johnson for Signing the Civil Rights Bill, the NAACP, Walton Cronkite, Barbara Walters, Jim Thorpe, Jesse Owens, Althea Gibson, Jim Brown, Willie Mays, Mickey Mantle, Pete Rose, Billy Jean, King, Oscar Robertson, Earl Monroe, Bill Russell, Paul Newman, Sarah Vaughn, Bill Cosby. I think you get the picture, I can write another book just on heroes. None of the aforementioned people were perfect, but there is and was something good in all of them. We as people, young and old, can learn from others regardless of their backgrounds. Today you young people have all of my heroes, the ones I didn't mention, as well as the First Family. The first Latino Supreme Court Justice, Sonia Sotomayor. LL Cool J, a performer who married his high school sweet heart and has a lovely family. We can sit back and make millions of excuses of why we cannot live up to our personal fatherly or motherly responsibilities, but there is absolutely no reason on God's green earth for us to not be personally responsible for our actions. While writing this book and other manuscripts, what inspires me is the number of mother and fathers who take their children to the library. Do you have a library card? I can hardly write unless I do it at a library. That's one of the only places I can concentrate, and I must admit that I got my first library card to get my daughter a book for her class back in the late nineties or early 2000's. Young ladies and gentleman, don't make excuses. Make your mom and dad proud and better yet, make something of yourself. I wish my mother could be alive today to see the progress of her remaining grandchildren. The prospect of her son becoming an author, novelist and screenplay writer. One of my biggest heroes is the incomparable Oprah Winfrey. This is a woman who had very humble beginnings but is now one of the wealthiest and most powerful women in the world. Ms. Winfrey is an example to women worldwide of all colors, she empowers women to go achieve and be a leader and not a follower. She created her own empire in such a short period of time and is worth over 2 billion dollars. Walter Cronkite, one of the most respected journalist ever. I remember Mr. Cronkite announcing the assignation of President Kennedy. He was the person that people wanted to get their news from. He was the one people trusted. Choose your own heroes young people. Geraldo Rivera is another hero. He was first on hand for many natural disasters throughout the years. On his TV show "Geraldo", he covered many topics of concern at the time. Mr. Rivera speaks his mind and I find him to be balanced and honest in his judgments on many topics. He wrote a book on the good and the bad in his life. That is hard for anyone. Not to mention the amount of years he spent in front of the camera. For his longevity, intelligence, and bravery in the assignments he took on, he is one of my all-time heroes. The forty-third President of the United States, George W. Bush, had a look on his face that I will never forget once he received word about the terrorist acts that took place on September 11, 2001. This national tragedy affected the world at large, our financial system, and the financial markets around the world. I don't think anyone in their right mind would have voluntarily traded places with President Bush. Politics aside, this was a time to pull together not only as a nation, but also as a world. I was in the great city of New York at the time. I had just dropped my daughter off at school. While sitting at a traffic light and listening to the news, there was a newsbreak that an airplane had just struck one of the Twin Towers. I literally lowered the window in my car and looked up in the sky to see if there were any clouds or fog to cause something like this. Of course, I kept the radio on the news and by the time I got home the other tower was hit. By then I knew it was a terrorist attack. You didn't have to be a brain surgeon to figure that out. The President came to ground-zero with the Governor and Mayor of New York and re-assured the world that those who committed that horrific crime would have to pay the price. This country lost three thousand lives that day, and for over the next seven years this country did not suffer another attack. My brother lost a neighbor on 9/11, a member of my daughter's school's teaching staff lost a friend as well. My wife worked two blocks away from ground-zero. The smell of ash reached beyond where I worked my second job on 86th street and 2nd avenue. In all of my years of following and keeping my eyes on Presidents, this had to be one of the hardest periods for any President. President Bush seemed to have kept the country on alert to avoid any other possible attacks. For that, this country is grateful. As young men, there are many heroes that can be looked up to. Will Smith, a young man who became an actor, rapper, husband, and father, came from humble beginnings. Born and raised in a working class family, he went on to have a successful music career, and an even more successful career in television and film. Will Smith is a man who takes his family life and career very seriously. Paul Newman, an actor for all ages, prospered in areas of comedy, drama, and action. He also created a salad dressing and donated the proceeds to charity. Mr. Newman made a string of incredible movies; it would take me a whole other book just to name all the exceptional movies that he made in his career. All of his contributions really add up. Tyra Banks is a perfect example of the complete woman. She's young, self-made, and an advocate for young women of all backgrounds. She helps empower women to be at the top of their game and she helps them with not only words, but action. She received a call from President Obama to congratulate her on her 100th show and also thanked her for being a positive role model for men and women. Ms. Banks is truly an example for women of all ages to look up to. Another example of a person who gives back in a large way and is an advocate for the needy, Angelina Jolie. She and her husband, Brad Pitt, are true advocates for reaching out to others and are the perfect examples of celebrities who have the financial resources and time to help others. You may wonder why am I writing about these wealthy celebrities, and the reason is because these wealthy celebrities are not obligated to help others. They could remain in their comfort zone and could care less about the disadvantaged. But for those with much, much is expected. Take for example U2's Bono, George Clooney, and former President George W. Bush. Their contributions and advocacy for the continent of Africa, makes them heroes. Young people have to become responsible in their personal lives and towards the children that you have. We can do it, there is a lot we can do if we put our best foot forward. Don't limit yourselves. Look at LL Cool J. Started as a teen hip-hop artist, movie star, and married his high school sweet heart. In addition, let me also mention that he has started a clothing line and maintained his sex symbol status since the 1980s. He is a family man, a health advocate, and a person that was never connected to the rough and tough side of the rap game. Many times when we think of heroes, we think of famous people. However, many heroes are not famous, or are unsung heroes. For example, teachers, community activist, doctors, and business owners to name a few. Sheryl Lee Ralph is a major advocate for HIV and AIDS prevention and is on the front lines when it comes to this issue. She should be congratulated for her advocacy and dedication. I had the privilege and pleasure to meet an MD who is an advocate for HIV and AIDS as well as an Assistant Commissioner in New York City. Her name is Dr. Monica Sweeney. I met her at a seminar on HIV/AIDS and she was terrific. Dr. Sweeney urged the audience to be responsible in our sexual behavior, and if having sex, use condoms. She has been referred to as the condom queen, because of her book Condom Sense. Nationwide, 1/3 of young women will be pregnant by the age of twenty. Another staggering statistic is that 1 in 5 kids will have sex by age fifteen. We need people like Dr. Sweeney in our communities across the country fighting for our young people. Dr. Laura Berman of the Oprah Winfrey Show, had an episode to help two fourteen-year-old kids to think about not having sex. Dr. Berman answered questions and counseled the young man's mother about buying her son condoms. It was a pleasure to see that at the end of the show, that a young woman got a standing ovation for having second thoughts about having sex at age fourteen. I've seen too many shows that have people regretting that they have become parents way too soon. Once again, it takes parental involvement. One of my other heroes is General Colin Powell. Born and raised in the Bronx, he came from humble beginnings. His family made sure that he stayed focused and advised him that going to college was his only option. The life of General Colin Powell is common; just not to the same height; that is ordinary, regular people becoming outstanding people in the community. After his life long commitment to the public sector, he is an advocate of empowering young men and women to achieve their best in life, and to be responsible and to challenge themselves. There are plenty of heroes in our nation's school sector who go beyond the call of duty. Many of us see the need to push young people to understand that education is the great equalizer. Education gives each of us a better chance to get a better job and make more money. The average student with a college education earns at least one million dollars more than a person without one. There are people who I may never match up to, who have given their heart, soul, and every fiber of their being to the betterment of our young people. There are three such people that deserve our praise and appreciation due to their undeniable dedication to our young adults. Starting with the wife of comedian Chris Rock, Mrs. Malaak Rock. This lovely woman takes thirty young men and women from the Bushwick Salvation Army in Brooklyn, to South Africa every year. The purpose of the trip is to encourage the kids to try harder to achieve their goals and to be grateful

*The whole gang.*

of what they do have. They spend two weeks observing the living conditions and differences in lifestyle there versus here in the United States. They also have the honor of meeting the legendary Bishop Desmond Tutu. After the thirty-six hour round trip, the kids showed improvement and gave back to their Brooklyn community. Malaak Rock could have easily enjoyed the perks of her wealth, but instead decided to give back to her community. Another example exists in the state of Connecticut with Mr. Steve Perry. This is a self-made educator who worked himself up, took personal responsibility for his life, and climbed to the mountaintop. Here is a man who grew up in the housing projects, had his fair share of problems as a youth, but got his act together and earned a bachelor's degree in social work. He went on to earn a PhD. Dr. Steve Perry went on to open The Capitol Prep Magnet School in Hartford Connecticut. He serves as the principal of the school and assist in picking students up, waking up at 4:45 AM everyday, as well as greeting them every morning when school starts. With the support of his devoted wife, he maintains a six-day a work week, year round to assure these children have the best chance of achievement. Some of the students have family issues at home that may interfere with their chances of becoming successful adults. With a program entitled "Strategy for Success", the school offers college courses and has a 100% graduation rate. The entire staff at The Capitol Prep Magnet School deserves our acknowledgement for the great job they are doing with the youth in Hartford. Collectively, they truly are an inspiration to us all. Mr. Jeff Canada, another man who was willing to overcome odds and reach out to our youth. Mr. Canada was born and raised in the Bronx, and he saw the need to put his community at the forefront. By working with 10,000 children each year, and doing so within a 100-block radius in Harlem, he was able to start the Harlem Children's Zone. The Harlem Children's Zone has Baby College Programs, Pre-school programs, as well as foreign language courses. He urges children's education must start at birth. The school was recently credited with having the smartest 4th grade students in the entire state of New York. The charter school rewards children with trips to Disney World. With all that said, parents must be involved in their children's lives. At Mr. Perry's school, there are times where there are more teachers in the stands at the school's athletic events than parents. Unfortunately, the case may be that the parents are incarcerated, working two jobs, or in some cases just don't care. I want to thank Ms. Solidad O'Brian and CNN for their continued focus on our young and disadvantaged adults. Every so often, you work with people who are related to unsung heroes. I know one such person whose father was a hero to her. The person's name is Janet Collado-Ortiz. Mr. Collado suffered from diabetes and his ability to work was affected by the disease. Ms. Collado becomes the breadwinner. Mr. Collado became Janet's confidant, mentor, walked her to school, and did her hair. He was also there to understand her change to womanhood. This wonderful father passed away but left a great impression on her life even to this day. Janet Collado-Ortiz has fond memories of her dad. Mr. Collado is a hero to his daughter and to all good fathers everywhere. Janet is a wonderful woman and a wonderful mother to her children. Let us keep

in mind that 40% of all births are out of wedlock, 42% of those births are by African American individuals.

Other heroes exist in the business and political sector, like Dr. Susan and John Rice. Dr. Rice is a veteran who served in President Bill Clinton's State department and now serves in President Barack Obama's administration. Mr. John Rice, Chairman and CEO of the company MLT out of Atlanta Georgia, is a wonderful company helping to reshape and train people to be effective in the corporate world, qualifying us to be the best. These two brilliant people, who happen to be African American, are a credit to the world community. While traveling, you can meet everyday heroes as well, which has happened to me. Another unsung hero is Jeanette Sassy Withers. Jeanette was born and raised in Birmingham Alabama by her parents along with her brother and seven sisters. Her parents educated them on the importance of using birth control and preventing unwanted pregnancies. Her father did not allow men hanging around his daughters. At age seventeen, Jeanette moved to New York. She joined the Army Reserves and while with them, she worked for the New York City Fire department and became a member of the union DC-37. Ms. Withers is a twenty-five year member of DC-37, twenty-three year member of the Army Reserves, and a thirty-year employee of the New York City Fire department. There is a song by the legendary Chaka Khan called "I'm every woman" and Ms. Withers is truly every woman. The life and times of Sassy Withers is an example of how both men and women should stay focused and not be fooled by what's popular to the world at large, as well as looking at the big picture. There is a judge out of Detroit Michigan, Wayne McCree, who runs a "Deadbeat Dad Center". In the state of Michigan, deadbeat fathers get four years in prison for not supporting their kids. The state as a whole is cracking down on irresponsible parents. To help young families, many programs on TV are trying to keep families together. In Chicago, a pool of doctors started the "Project Brotherhood". These black inner city doctors saw the need to reach out to men of color and stress to them the importance of regular doctor visits. They would visit barbershops, local parks, anywhere in the neighborhood that men would gather. For these doctors to reach out in this matter, they must be commended. There are thousands of heroes that could be acknowledged, but you get the point. I mentioned heroes of every shape and form. In this life, it boils down to us individually and our own options. Now the question is what are you going to do? How are going to live your life? As young ladies, are you going to take responsibility for your own bodies? Young men, are you going to take the time to get focused and work on being a man? Are you going to love and respect the gift called woman? There are absolutely no excuses. The great movie "The Pursuit of Happiness" featured the life of Chris Gardner. Gardner said his life of being homeless and out of work had more to do with being a good father than going from rags to riches. It's about being a family man or woman. Mr. Gardner and his son were portrayed by Will Smith and his son on film. His book, Start Where You Are, I am sure will urge us to never give up. Unfortunately, life can

*A time to give thanks.*

*Mom and her boys.*

be like a game of dominoes. When men for decades turn their backs on the family, it would not take long for woman to follow suit. In the August 2009 issue of Marie Claire magazine, on page eighty-four, there was an article titled "What kind of mother leaves her kids"? The story featured three women who left their families and their children. One of the questions posed by the women asked why men who leave their families after a divorce are viewed differently than women who do the same thing. It is up to us as men to get a handle on this widening problem. Reaffirm our responsibilities as heads of our households and be there for our families whole-heartedly. Men, there is no better joy than to get a call from your appreciative kids for being an active father. No money in the world can possibly replace such a feeling. Many years ago, my late sister Chantel called my oldest brother Harold a king, which is a compliment out of respect for him. I in turn call my oldest son "top dog", my second son "big dog", and my daughter "princess". There are names of endearment, reassurance, and love. The practice of pet names worked for us, give it a try. Try anything that works. I want to thank you readers of this book. This book was hard to write because it brought up many memories of my incredible mother Gladys Russell. Truly a legend for all times, and the primary reason for me writing this book. Thank you momma! The last but not least hero of this book is the young people. Each of you have the chance, ability, and purpose to succeed. Don't miss the opportunity. Be the best young adults you can be. Use my humble life story, as well as my families as an example that you can do it. Believe in yourselves. While working with a young man, we struck up a discussion about today's youth and he asked who made me an authority on young people's concerns? My answer, I'm not an authority. I don't have a degree. This book was designed to tell a story of a father and mother who came from working class backgrounds and devoted their time and efforts to raise their children as best as they possibly could. I speak from experience.

The second question that may come up, what should a young lady do that has become pregnant. In the book, I stressed the importance of abstinence and having protected sex, but I also stress talking to your parents and be responsible. These are only my answers and suggestions.

For those that are already teen-aged dads, you may wonder if you should find work or go to college. My answer for you is that your primary responsibility is to the child and the child's mother, and you both must put that child's interest first.

For young men or women who want to be parents now at a young age, just know that you can't expect to live the same life you live now without children.

I also stress in the book for men and women to wait until they have children, at least until they are between the ages of twenty-two or twenty-five. On average, you would have completed four years of college and you would have become more well rounded and mature. Being parents is not an easy job. My wife was a teenaged mother and I was just twenty-four without a college education. We struggled unnecessarily. We should have waited and saved more money, or even gone to college. All we had was each other and we learned the hard way.

As a young lady, if you become pregnant, then you and the father of the child need to make decisions together. If you are under aged, then talking to your parents or a counselor is what I recommend.

In the book, I strongly encourage all of our youth to be law-abiding citizens and avoid jail at all cost. Once you are incarcerated, there is no way that you can support your family.

My wife and I manage to teach our children to avoid the drama associated with having children out of wedlock. We both grew up religious and we taught them by example of what path they should take towards having children.

In the book, I mentioned an article in Marie Claire about mothers who abandoned their families. Young adults may ask how can this be avoided, and the best answer I can give is to get to know the person you are involved with. Become friends first, start a relationship, get married. Following these steps could cut down on broken homes.

Finally, for those fathers who wonder how they can be the best father they can be, I tell them that it is very simple. You must be committed, make it a point to appreciate the greatest gift from God, which is the woman. As a man, you wouldn't cut off your arm, your tongue, or any other body part so don't do the same harm to our women. Cherish your woman. And love her like no other. A young lady once told me that she wants a man to love her like he won't be able to live without her. I always liked that expression, young ladies this is an expression and feeling that must go both ways. Take the time to be friends and then life partners. Thank You!

P.S.: Don't forget you folks to live by this rule "A winner never quits and a quitter never wins". Fellas, be a "Be there Father". Be a Winner!

A Special Reminder To All Fathers: Gentlemen, our sons follow our lead, our daughters learn to trust, admire and love their first male heroes, their Dads. We have to earn sons leadership, our own daughters trust we can't do that, "by not being there." A message from the president of the United States, Barack Obama: Children are twenty times likely to go to a person without their fathers a home, fine time to in poverty. Last but not least, nine times to drop out of school. So fathers, we have a lot of work to do.

# Hero — Lebron James

While watching the Charlie Rose show, I was blown away at this young athlete's rise to the top of the NBA (sharing the spot with Kobe Bryant and Dwayne Wade) in the period of six years. At the age of seventeen years old, he made the cover of Sports Illustrated, graduated from high school, and had enough talent to go straight to the NBA. I've never seen such hoopla before in my life. But this book is not about his unbelievable career thus far, this book is about people being in position to give back and not forgetting where you come from. Mr. James is only twenty-four years old, from a single parent home, and he says that his mother supported his basketball aspirations. She told him "Go for it". Born and raised in Akron Ohio, he credits his basketball career to Coach Drew and having his four friends, who tell him the non-sugar coated truth and are not yes men. On 60 Minutes, it was reported that his life long friends help him with his business affairs and negotiations. He is the father of one son, and yes, he is a "Be There" father. He refuses to have his son grow up without a father. Young ladies and gentleman, don't just look at Lebron as just the basketball hero, but as an example of being a responsible parent. Make him your hero on and off the court, he makes my special hero award (by the way, he will get his first ring this year with Shaq).

## Special Note

Unfortunately, after thirty-one years of marriage, both Loretta and I decided to end our marriage. It's a decision I'm still dealing with. We're the best of friends and are extremely proud of our family's accomplishments.

# Special, Special, Special Thanks!

First, I want to thank my oldest son, for being a great example to his younger brother and sister. Lanard was told right before his 30th birthday, that his book, "Father's Day", was conceived because of his great leadership as the oldest. He also, while working a full time job, came home at night and put his father's hundreds and hundreds of hand written pages of his manuscript on the computer. Thank you son so much!

Second- I want to give a special thanks to Terrance, for loving and respecting his older brother's example, and for being a good example to his younger sister, Ashley.

Third, but not last. I thank my baby daughter Ashley, for listening and respecting the leadership of her two older brothers. She also, is the oldest granddaughter on her father's side, and is a good example to her younger female cousins.

All three of my children, were nice enough to contribute to their father's first book, their mother and I are very happy with all three of their lives.

# About the Author

What qualifies Theodore Wentz to write about being a successful father? Like our forty-fourth President, and millions of other children who were victims of being abandoned by one or both of their parents, this is an indescribable emptiness that will take you to your grave. In his case, it was his father who abused his mother, and his mother had to put him out for drinking and not being an example to his children. He'll never for as long as he lives forget her words "I'll raise these kids myself before I let you not be a positive role model to your boys". His mother, to whom this book is dedicated, made the choice to do it alone, with five boys and one daughter from his father. She began working one or two jobs if necessary to feed, clothe, provide shelter, and raise them, believing in God and attending their local congregation and seeking the help of their elders in their congregation. In writing this book, he bring to the table a life long example of hard work, love for family, and a high respect for our most precious gift from God, our women. Theodore can look any young man and woman in the eye and tell them, with 31 years of parental experience, about seeing the value of being raised by a "be there" mom and that of his life experiences can help them be a responsible parent. No PHD of any kind could replace that wealth of experience.

www.ingramcontent.com/pod-product-compliance
Lightning Source LLC
Chambersburg PA
CBHW021545290526
45785CB00004BA/1520